21 Days to a *Thrifty* Lifestyle

Books in the 21-Day Series

Proven Plan
for Beginning
New Habits

21 Days to a *Thrifty* Lifestyle

Mike Yorkey

Series Editor
Dan Benson

ZondervanPublishingHouse
Grand Rapids, Michigan

A Division of HarperCollins*Publishers*

CONTENTS

DISCLAIMER

This publication is designed to provide sound and helpful information in regard to the subject matter covered. It is sold with the understanding that neither the author, nor the series editor, nor the publisher is engaged in rendering legal, investment, accounting, or other professional advice or services.

Because every reader's financial situation and goals are unique, it is recommended that a financial professional be consulted prior to implementing any of the suggestions in this book.

INTRODUCTION

SAVING MONEY CAN BE TOUGH

This book will help you save money on everyday household expenses, but I have to be honest with you: This "saving money" business can be tough.

I don't know about you, but it seems like whenever my wife, Nicole, and I have squirreled away a little money . . . blam! we get blindsided by another big car-repair bill.

But that's all right. Nicole and I know that God is in control—although I worry way too much as the father of two children, Andrea, fourteen, and Patrick, thirteen. Perhaps that's because I *know* too much. A couple of years ago I began tracking our finances on the family computer, and in 1996 the Yorkey family spent 97.2 percent of everything that came in. As you can see, our margin of error was razor thin, but at least we didn't spend *more* than we earned (something that's happened a couple of times over nearly twenty years of marriage).

Life continues to be a financial scramble in our household, as I imagine it is in yours. It's my belief that today's American families—overtaxed and squeezed by stagnant pay—are barely keeping their noses above water. Many of us are living paycheck to paycheck and bracing ourselves for the next calamity—such as a broken furnace. And who knows how we're going to pay for our next car, our children's college educations, and our looming retirement.

Thus, the pressure to live within our means can place tremendous stresses on everyone. That's why saving money on basic household expenses, such as food, clothing, housing, education, and health care can result in a net savings of $200 to $300 a month—often the difference between a family's staying above the waterline or sinking further into debt.

What expertise do I bring to the table? Well, I've been editor of *Focus on the Family* magazine since 1986, and a good chunk of my workday is spent reading and writing about today's families. In 1994, I wrote *Saving Money Any Way You Can* (Servant) because I thought families need a resource filled with *practical* ideas on how families can save money on everyday expenses. That book did well, and since its release I've continued to scour newspapers and magazines to keep myself abreast of the saving-money landscape.

I am amazed to see some significant changes since I wrote *Saving Money Any Way You Can*. Just a few years ago, the Internet was some far-out thing for computer tekkies. Now, more and more families are using the Net to send mail and conduct research, and Internet commerce is being invented before our eyes.

Each Wednesday, for example, American Airlines and TWA post new fares on unsold seats for the coming weekend. Are they a good deal? Does that mean we should wait until the last minute to purchase an "e-ticket" instead of booking twenty-one days in advance for the best rate? (You'll find those answers on Day 14.)

But we're getting ahead of ourselves here. In the coming pages, you'll discover that I've written *21 Days to a Thrifty Lifestyle* in quick bursts that will arm you with sufficient knowledge to be a good shopper.

One thing you should know right from the beginning: I am not a tightwad. You won't find advice on cutting up old shower curtains and turning them into baby bibs, or collecting clothes dryer lint and making your own stuffed animals. Instead, my goal is to help you save a few dollars here and there on everyday family purchases, a practice that can help you stay out of debt.

But there's another aspect to keep in mind. Saving money on household items may allow you and your family to support that missionary family that you met on furlough, or let you financially respond when your church announces a building drive. The Lord delights in our gifts—not because he needs them, but because we are faithful in supporting his work.

The Lord also delights when we look to him before making an important buying decision, so make major purchases part of your prayer time. Ask Christ to open or close the door on a deal to purchase a used car. Ask Christ to help you find a good, used bunk bed in the want ads.

Remember how I mentioned that I worry too much? If you're like me, then let's hold close to Jesus' words from Matthew 6:25–26 (TLB): "So my counsel is: Don't worry about *things*— food, drink, and clothes. For you already have life and a body— and they are far more important than what to eat and wear. Look at the birds! They don't worry about what to eat . . . for your heavenly Father feeds them. And you are far more valuable to him than they are."

Nope, we don't have too much to worry about. We just have to do our part by looking for good deals and knowing *when* we're getting a good deal. This book will help you do that.

DAY 1

Make My Budget Supersize

A good spending plan is like a spoonful of good medicine

For the past few years, I've been a guest speaker on saving money at the Focus on the Family Institute. Each semester, I stand before forty bright college students who've come to Focus on the Family's Colorado Springs campus for five months of intensive family-related classes and tell them my story.

"Several years ago, Nicole and I purchased our first home in southern California, a thirty-year-old tract home that needed a new roof," I begin. "We did our best to fix up the place, doing all the work ourselves, but just after the New Year, I had a sinking feeling that we had been spending more than we had been earning all year long. In fact, we were down to a couple thousand dollars in our savings account, and unless we made a quick turnaround we would be incurring some big-time debt. That's when I decided to go back and piece together our first year of home ownership as best I could.

"I picked up a spiral notebook and made out pages for groceries, gas purchases, clothes, car repairs, sports equipment—anything I could think of. Then I went through our checkbook, credit card statements, and all the receipts we had saved, writing down the amounts in the notebook. When all was said and done, we had spent $2,500 *more* than we brought in that year."

I have the students' attention now.

"I took Nicole out to our favorite Chinese restaurant and shared what I had learned with her," I continue. "We both agreed that changes were in order, so we began cutting back where we could and stretching our dollars. The following year, we showed a family profit, if you will, of $1,200."

The students usually register mild interest at that point. "That works out to $100 a month," I say, "which isn't much, folks."

Then I walk to the blackboard. "In a few months or perhaps a year or two, you will be graduating from college, getting your first job, and living on your own. Let's take a look at what that's going to cost."

In large block letters, I write: RENT. "What are you going to have to pay for rent?" I ask the class.

"Three hundred dollars," yells one student.

"No way I'd live in a place that cheap," chimes in a young woman. "Eight hundred dollars."

"You're spoiled," retorts a male. "I could find a place for $400."

I still haven't written a figure behind RENT. Dr. Michael Rosebush, who invited me to speak to these students, jumps in.

"Class, the apartments you're living in off-campus cost us $1,100 a month."

A murmur sweeps the room. *That's $550 a month for each student.*

I write $550 behind RENT and move on to groceries. Some think they can eat for $75 a month, while others are sure they will have to spend $400. I jot down a middle figure: $200. From there, we take thirty minutes filling in numbers for the rest of the categories: utilities, clothes, phone, car insurance and repairs, restaurants, fast food, cable TV, Internet hookup, health insurance, haircuts, recreation, and miscellaneous.

Then I step over to another part of the blackboard and write down the take-home pay for $9 an hour, $12 an hour, and $15 an hour—pretty decent wages for someone just getting out of college. When we compare the "outgo" with the "in-go," incredulous looks cover the students' faces. Those making $9 an hour have no chance; those earning $12 would break even; and those earning $15 would be living on Easy Street.

"The problem is that many of you will not be able to earn $9 an hour with your first job," I explain.

Dr. Rosebush backs me up. "In case you're wondering, class, over half the support staff here at the Focus on the Family Institute aren't making $9 an hour."

Talk about depressing.

"Oh, one more thing is missing here," I point out. "We haven't even put down your tithe."

All the air is sucked out of the room.

While that little exercise is always an eye-opener for the college students, I wonder how many families know where their financial ship is sailing. Christian financial counselors have told me that very few couples have a budget and actually follow it.

I understand why, because Nicole and I do not have a formal budget either. Budgets are a hassle, involve a lot of time, and are no fun. Besides, how can you foresee the need to repair a sprinkler system or replace a broken dishwasher, refrigerator, and washing machine—which happened in our household last year?

The answer is, by budgeting for those repairs. I guess—putting aside monies for the "worst-case" scenarios. With each passing year, I see how budgets provide clear financial goals, keep you from overspending, and can actually be freeing.

I've taken some intermediate steps to get there. I've prepared a family budget detailing what we can expect to pay for our mortgage, utilities, groceries, car repairs, charitable giving, and so forth. We use Quicken personal-finance software to track our expenses. (That sure beats my old spiral notebooks.)

Whenever we have a "bad month"—usually a big car repair—we cut back in other areas or delay purchases to see us through. It's not by the book, but it's worked for us.

Since I'm not an expert on budgeting, I sought out Mahlon Hetrick, president of a ministry called Christian Financial Counseling in Fort Myers, Florida (941–337–2122), and author of *The Money Workbook* (Barbour, 1993).

Q: **What's one of the biggest mistakes you see couples making with their finances?**

Mahlon: I see way too many families who have no budget, no spending plan, no savings, too much credit, too much overspending, and wanting too much too soon.

Q: **Hmmm, that kind of says it all. What's the first thing couples should do to introduce themselves to budgeting?**

Mahlon: Proverbs 18:13 says, "What a shame—yes, how stupid!—to decide before knowing the facts!" (TLB). The first thing couples need to do is gather the facts. You need to know how much you are paying for rent or your mortgage, what your car expenses are, and all the other household expenditures. You need to know your tax situation. Often we discover people who are over-withholding. All they're doing is giving the IRS their money to hold before its returned to them with no interest. That's not wise.

But the biggest problem we see is a lack of discipline with credit card use. That's why they overspend.

Q: **How much credit card debt are we talking about?**

Mahlon: Anywhere from $15,000 to $50,000. Sometimes even more. But you know, it doesn't matter how much income a family brings in. If you overspend with a household income of $20,000, you'll overspend with a household income of $50,000.

Q: **It's been estimated that only 5 percent of couples have a budget. Is that what you're seeing?**

Mahlon: I sure am. Most people think they have a budget, but what we find is that people are record keepers. They don't have a budget. They keep track of what comes in and goes out.

Let's assume that your outgo exceeds your income by $600 a month. If I were to ask you what the problem is, you would tell me that your outgo exceeds your income.

If I were to ask you in which category you're doing well or which area you're overspending, you'd have no idea. You wouldn't have any idea until you have a written guideline that tells you what you can afford to spend for your level of income.

Q: **So you're saying that without putting things down in writing, you can't identify what's causing the problem.**

Mahlon: That's right. You see, people do not usually have a money problem. They have an ignorance problem about money matters. They have not been taught guidelines for spending in the various budget categories based on their level of income. They also have attitude problems about money—problems with pride, greed, coveting, and so forth. The average family spends about 110 percent of their income, living beyond their means.

By God's standard, we are not wise, since Proverbs 21:20 tell us, "The wise man saves for the future, but the foolish man spends whatever he gets" (TLB). If we lived according to this proverb, we would eliminate 95 percent of all our money problems. But we're not listening to God. People don't understand that the Bible is the best book on finances ever written. Look at Proverbs 2:1–10 to learn how to make right decisions every time.

Q: **So what's the bottom line here for our readers?**

Mahlon: You can listen to God or listen to the world. It's your choice. God's answer will allow you to provide better for your family, save for the future, pay your bills on time, eliminate worry and frustration, and honor him with your tithe.

Everyone wants a quick fix, but there's no such thing. Boiled down, there are only three things you can do:

1. Increase income
2. Lower your outgo
3. Control your future spending

You need to make a list of ways to accomplish these things. You need to be creative and put on your thinking cap. Start by making a list of everything you will need to buy in the next month and stick to that list. Don't carry checks or credit cards. Carry only the cash needed for that day's planned spending. That helps eliminate impulse spending.

If you choose to be a good manager, God has good news for you: He will return a blessing greater than expected. "For God, who gives seed to the farmer to plant, and later on, good crops to harvest and eat, will give you more and more seed to plant and will make it grow so that you can give away more and more fruit from your harvest" (2 Cor. 9:10).

What better thing to bank on than God's Word?

Mahlon didn't pull any punches, did he? With his advice ringing in our ears, let's dive into the family's second-largest expenditure (after housing)—food.

LESSON OF THE DAY

*Although few families have a budget, you
have to know what's coming in and what's
going out. Otherwise, you're destined to
spend more than you earn.*

Supermarket Sweep

You can beat the supermarkets at their own game

Why is it that when I walk into a large supermarket, I have to make a right turn and push my cart to the far right wall to buy lettuce and tomatoes?

And why do I then have to push my cart along the back of the store *all* the way to the other side of the 60,000-square-foot building just to find a gallon of milk?

The answer is because supermarket interior designers want me to pass their "end caps," or featured items at the end of each aisle. If they can entice me to drop something in my cart that I wasn't planning to buy—say, two boxes of Cheerios—then it's advantage Safeway. The fact is, Cheerios weren't really on sale, but I couldn't comparison shop since the rest of the cereals were three aisles over.

Whether we know it or not, the supermarket world is a carefully orchestrated shopping experience, and we are unwitting participants.

"Supermarket designers know your heart," wrote Jack Hitt in the *New York Times Magazine*. "Their layout is a chaotic opera of flattery, soothing you with a wealth of options, making you feel that you're a chef picking over the finest meats, the most delicate in fresh greens, the best in imported condiments, even as your cart fills with familiar hamburger meat and iceberg lettuce, prepared cake mixes, and maybe that new frozen popcorn shrimp you've heard about."

In a thirty-minute shopping excursion, I will encounter more than 1,000 products, and it seems as though half those items end up in my cart. Seriously, there's a reason why supermarkets put their most profitable departments—produce, meat, deli, and seafood—around the perimeter, and that's because we must push our carts along the perimeter to get anywhere.

Delis—with their tantalizing displays of fresh cheese, thinly sliced mesquite turkey breast, delectable shrimp, and colorful salads—account for only 5 percent of a store's sales but 15 percent of the profits. Another profit center is cereal, which is arranged by brand rather than by type (again, to make it tougher to compare prices). It's no mistake that sweetened cereals—Froot Loops, Corn Pops, and Frosted Flakes—are at knee-level, right where your little children can grab a box.

To level the playing field, here are some strategies:

1. Know your prices. One time, you should type out a list of grocery staples and comparison shop the supermarkets you like to frequent. Have a good attitude: it can be fun once. You should compare the prices of your favorite cereals, ketchup, peanut butter, jam, hamburger meat, milk, bread, toilet tissue, paper towels, cough syrup, and so forth, at two or three supermarkets, plus a warehouse club (if you have one nearby).

My comparison shopping tests have shown that if I spent $135 at our local "bag your own groceries" chain, the same groceries cost $150 at our neighborhood upscale supermarket, about an 11 percent difference. That translates to around $800 annually if you spend the national average of $600 per month for a family of four.

What about warehouse clubs for groceries? While warehouse clubs have their limitations, you can save big bucks on groceries—around 33–48 percent. I'll talk more about warehouse clubs on Day 4.

2. Work your shopping list. According to the Point-of-Purchase Advertising Institute, consumers buy nearly twice as many items as they intend to buy. This is good news and bad news. On the one hand you want to fill your cart when there's a good sale on. On the other hand, "splurchases" of oversized blueberry muffins, Ding-Dongs, and Häagen-Dazs chocolate bars make the cash register ring *chi-ching*.

Also, it's not a good idea to shop when you're hungry, unless it's a Saturday and the supermarket has all those tasty samples to try.

3. Follow the loss leaders. Each week, loss leaders are bannered in the supermarkets' advertising flyers inserted into your Wednesday newspaper or mailed to your home. Loss leaders are products sold at cost or a few cents below, with the idea that you'll come into the store to buy them and fill the cart with the rest of your weekly shopping. A week before the Fourth of July, for instance, you'll find "firecracker" savings on spare ribs, barbecue sauce, and twelve-packs of Coke.

If that's the case, then perhaps the Fourth of July is not the time to serve a juicy filet mignon, since that is not discounted from its everyday price of $5.98 a pound. Instead, go with the ribs and save that filet mignon for when it goes on sale.

You can also "cherry pick" loss leaders from supermarkets you normally don't frequent. When it's been convenient, I've stopped many times at our upscale supermarket to load up on sale items only.

4. Check out store brands. These days I have a pretty good handle on the regular prices of my favorite national brands: Tropicana orange juice, Dannon yogurt, Dryer's ice cream, and Kellogg's Mueslix cereal, to name a few.

Store brands (or private labels) for the same products are cheaper—30 percent in most cases—and on many items the differences in taste and quality are indiscernible. I have no trouble drinking store-brand premium OJ (the not-from-concentrate kind), and the private-label mueslix-type cereal is delicious—and nearly $2 less a box.

But the herd mentality prevails in many households. A Yankelovich Monitor poll showed that 75 percent of respondents agreed with this statement: "Once I find a brand I like, it is very difficult to get me to change brands."

Folks, this type of thinking has to change. Look for the in-aisle signs that say, "Compare to the national brand and save!" You will.

5. Take along your coupon stash. I'll get into coupons in the next chapter, but for now let me encourage you to use coupons as part of your shopping strategy. How deeply you want to get into coupons is your decision, but it's easy to find coupons for your favorite cereal, baby diapers, and personal care products. Also, look for the point-of-purchase coupons. Some have blinking lights to catch your attention. But careful! That name brand *with* a coupon may not be cheaper than the store brand.

6. When meat goes on sale, don't tarry. With so many meals built around meat, you have to jump on meat sales. My favorite is when boneless chicken breasts drop from $3.99 a pound to $1.99 a pound, which happens like clockwork every six to ten weeks. We buy a dozen or two packages for the freezer and use the chicken for everything from stir-fry to chicken parmesan.

We have an old refrigerator in the garage to stash our bargains, but we haven't forgotten that freezer burn can hit after six months. Every now and then we'll have an "empty the fridge" week.

7. Skip the gourmet supermarkets. They're starting to sprout up in tony neighborhoods, and they go by names like Whole Foods, Fresh Fields, and Breads & Circus. But do you really need to pay $10 a pound for hormone-free steaks or $6 for a loaf of preservative-free bread? The desire to cut additives in our food is laudatory, but that's a lot of money to pay for food that is only marginally healthier for you.

8. Buy as few prepared foods as you can. You pay a premium for bags of prepared salad, baby carrots, macaroni salad, cole slaw, frozen dinners, and goodies from the bakery.

9. Don't be afraid to ask for a discount. Slightly bruised fruit and wilting vegetables can be heavily discounted since they are probably a day away from being thrown out, but you have to ask someone in the produce department. Believe me, they want it off the floor. Just ask, "What kind of discount could you give me if I purchase this bruised fruit?"

10. Ask for the rain checks. This is my favorite loss leader: When Dannon coffee yogurt, which normally cost 71 cents, goes down to three-for-a-dollar, I grab the last fifteen Dannon coffee yogurts from the shelf. Then at the cash register, I ask for a rain check, which means I can come back any time and purchase another cartload of coffee yogurts for 33 cents each!

11. Look for the "multi-buy" discounts. Many supermarket chains are discounting staples such as milk by offering a package deal. If you buy two gallons, then the cost is $4 instead of $2.75 for one gallon. Go for it.

12. Finally, take your time! Pushing a cart while juggling coupons and newspaper inserts, making price comparisons, looking for store brands, and wondering if a "sale" item is a bargain involves an investment in time. Remember, each time you make a good decision, you put a quarter or fifty cents or a dollar into your wallet, and you're earning money by being a savvy grocery shopper.

If you shop the loss leaders, use your coupons, and lay off the "splurchases," there's no reason why you can't save 20 percent, or $1,200 a year, on your food bill.

Clipping Coupons

Are they worth the hassle?

Paul Wilson knows coupons. Man, does he know coupons.

Paul is the author of *Real Men Use Coupons, Too!*, a member of the Coupon Council, and the inventor of the Coup-o-Dex, a rotary coupon file that you snap onto your shopping cart. When he appears on TV talk shows, he dresses in combat gear and takes on the persona of "Coupon Commando," who will lead the audience through "Supermarket Boot Camp."

When we chatted for this book, I admitted to Paul that I would be playing devil's advocate when it came to coupons. While I believe that coupons are an important part of grocery shopping strategy, I don't build my shopping *around* coupons. My ambivalent feelings match those of a growing number of shoppers: coupon distribution has steadily fallen since 1992, and 8 percent fewer coupons were redeemed in 1996 than the year before. The average face value also fell two cents the same year, to 67 cents, and expiration dates are tighter than ever—around three months.

Coupons are here to stay, however, because there's too much money at stake. Supermarkets like them because they bring people into the store and generate eight cents in handling charges. (Don't snicker; those little cents add up to over a half-billion dollars, since nearly seven billion coupons are redeemed each year.)

While consumers may blow hot and cold about coupons, more than 80 percent of us use coupons every month, according to an NCH Promotional Services Survey, and when Procter & Gamble test-marketed a no-coupon strategy in three upstate New York cities in early 1997, consumers rebelled. Coupons were reinstated pronto.

WHERE DO YOU START?

Your Sunday newspaper, which usually contains a 24-page circular for coupons, is where most grocery coupons are found, but few are worthy of being clipped and filed away. Let me walk you through the coupons in the first few pages of a recent Sunday insert I received:

- A $2 Boston Market coupon for any *two* individual meals. Sorry, but a buck off an already expensive-enough Boston Market quarter rotisserie chicken won't get me to bite.
- A 15-cent coupon for Mott's applesauce, 23 ounces or larger. Even doubling this coupon won't make this apple sauce cheaper than purchasing it at a warehouse club.
- A $1 coupon good for FoxVideos. Why would I want to buy *Sleeping with the Enemy* or *Waiting to Exhale* for $14 instead of $15?

- A 75-cent coupon for two eight-ounces-or-larger Kraft cheese products, such as Velveeta. Shop and compare: Store brand and warehouse club "Velveeta" are cheaper.
- A $3 coupon for a Brita water filtration pitcher. My Colorado tap water is just fine.
- A two-for-one coupon for Fancy Feast cat food. Sorry, we're a dog family.
- A 50-cent coupon when you buy *two* cans of Hormel Chunk Meat. Canned meat is expensive! I never buy it.
- A 50-cent coupon for any variety of Marrakesh Express Couscous. *C'est dommage*; we're not big lovers of couscous in our household.
- A 40-cent coupon when you buy any *two* packages of Hot Pockets stuffed sandwiches. That's only 20 cents off per box of overpriced frozen prepared foods.

And on and on it goes. Now, I will clip the cereal coupons (love those $1 coupons for Kellogg's Mueslix) and coupons for personal-care products such as toothpaste and shampoo, but I'm not going to go to the ends of the earth to find a $1 coupon for Balmex ointment for diaper rash.

HERE'S WHAT TO DO

If coupons are going to work, you need to hang around long enough to find the coupons for the type of products you use. "You'll have to leave brand loyalty at the door and try a different kind of paper towels once in a while," said Paul, the coupon man. "If you use a little discipline, saving 20 percent on groceries is not out of the question. Saving $10 with coupons is like saving $14, because you're not paying taxes on your time. You should be able to make $25 to $30 an hour without too much effort."

This is how the coupon game is played. First, you must collect coupons. That may sound simple, since more than 300 billion of the little chits are printed each year, but you'd be surprised how difficult it is to find *good* coupons. You'll have to look beyond the Sunday paper and hunt for coupons in the Thursday morning food section, in women's magazines such as *Good Housekeeping* or *Family Circle*, or visit the "coupon corner" found in many supermarkets, where you can take and trade.

Most supermarkets use the Catalina Marketing system, which prints out coupons at the checkout register, based on what you bought. For instance, if you purchased Minute Maid orange juice, the computer could spit out a 50-cent coupon for that product, or for a competitor's OJ, like Tropicana.

A local supermarket, King Soopers (part of Kroger), has taken the coupon game a step further. I signed up for a "SooperCard," which means that the in-store specials of the week are automatically reduced when I scan my card at check out. No need to clip and file, which I like.

You should also *ask* for coupons. Direct-mail coupon companies, such as Carol Wright, are a good resource, or you can fill out a Procter & Gamble product preference survey and get on P&G's formidable mailing list. (Write: Procter & Gamble, P.O. Box 5529, Cincinnati, OH 45201–5529.)

Paul Wilson takes this a step further by looking for the company's 800-number on the packages he's purchased.

"I call and ask the companies to put me on their mailing list for coupons," said Paul, "and they never refuse me. I also ask if they can send me coupons for different products they produce."

Once you stash your coupons in your little coupon organizer or Coup-o-Dex, it's time to be a shrewd shopper. (To order a Coup-o-Dex, which holds 1,000 coupons, call toll-free 800–268–7633. Cost is $24.50, which includes shipping.)

Buying the smallest size maximizes the coupon's value. Let's say you have a 50-cent coupon good for any size of Ban Roll-On. Purchase the tiny three-ounce bottle for $1.19, and if the store doubles the coupon, the net cost to you is only 19 cents.

You should also look for "double plays," or times when you can double the coupon's face value at the same time a supermarket puts the item on sale.

Here's the way it works. Let's say that A&P announces a "Buy One, Get One Free" sale on Prego spaghetti sauce. The cost for a 28-ounce jar is $2.29. At a two-for-one rate, the price has been cut in half, or $1.15. You take two 50-cent coupons out of your stash, which are doubled by A&P to $1 each. With $2 in refunds, your two jars of Prego cost you 29 cents.

So it's a game. Do you have a coupon for something that has gone on sale? Bingo! Even if you don't, you can still be handsomely rewarded for clipping a few coupons and buying name-brand products you don't normally purchase. Here are a few other ideas:

- Check out the newspaper recycling bins in the supermarket parking lots for coupon inserts. Look for the colored paper.
- Don't forget supermarket coupons. These are often loss leaders, and extra copies of the supermarket's inserts can usually be found in front of the store. If the store is running a coupon special on Raisin Bran but the shelf has been emptied, ask for a rain check.
- Be aware of co-branding coupons. This is the type of coupon with which you buy a loaf of bread and inside is a great coupon for grape jelly. Or a cereal box coupon allows you to buy a free gallon of milk or two pounds of bananas. Offbeat, but it works.
- Stay away from rebates unless they are $2 or more. Manufacturers make you work too hard to get a rebate; you

have to send in the original receipt, tear off part of the original packaging, fill out a form, and spend 32 cents in postage.

- If you are a couponer, the type of person who gets a rush buying Kraft Macaroni and Cheese with doubled coupons, then subscribe to *Refunding Makes Sense*. This monthly 100-page newsletter is crammed with the latest on coupons and rebates. (Write to: Refunding Makes Sense, Box R–839, Farmington, UT 84205. Cost is $25 a year.)

- Finally, keep those expired coupons—they can still be accepted. On several occasions I've gone through the checkout line with an expired coupon for my Mueslix. "This coupon expired last week, but will you still accept it?" I ask.

    I've never been refused. I figured that's because the supermarket wanted to make the customer happy. But then Paul Wilson told me that supermarkets have *three months* to redeem coupons with the manufacturers!

LESSON OF THE DAY

Don't leave home without your coupon organizer, and if you can make a "double play," go for it!

Get Thee to a Warehouse Club

But watch out: the more you buy, the more you save

Today we're going to gain an insider's look at warehouse clubs and show how you can use them to slash a third or half off your grocery bills.

Call it a blind spot, but I love warehouse clubs. Maybe that's because the nation's first warehouse club—the Price Club—opened in 1976 in my hometown of San Diego, and I've been shopping at them ever since. Sam's Clubs can be found nationwide, while Costcos are strong on the west and east coasts. BJ's, a regional East Coast outfit, is a minor league player.

They all look pretty much alike. I love the cavernous, bare-bones, low-rent atmosphere and forklifts stacking pallets of goods to the ceiling. Even the $25 annual membership fee doesn't bother me: *Hey, not just anybody can shop here*, I think.

But the real reason that warehouse clubs get my business is because I get a kick dropping a four-pound box of Grape Nuts into my cart and knowing that it costs 40 percent less than the same amount at a supermarket. A 40 percent savings is about average when shopping for groceries at warehouse clubs—unless the supermarket has made Grape Nuts a loss leader.

To help you understand why warehouse clubs offer consistent savings on everything from soup to nuts, from tires to small appliances, from TVs to refrigerators, and from batteries to film, I'm going to introduce Rich.

Rich and I have known each other for a while, and he's worked in the warehouse club industry for more than a decade.

Q: What's the average markup on merchandise?

Rich: The general markup is 8–8.5 percent. From that amount, we deduct payroll (4 percent), benefits (1.5 percent), utilities and supplies (.5 percent), taxes (1 percent), and central overhead and real estate (1 percent). All those expenses add up to 8 percent. Here's one of our bigger secrets: Without membership fees, Costco would not be profitable.

Q: You mean you don't make any money on the merchandise?

Rich: That's right. If it weren't for the annual membership fees, we couldn't stay in business. It can be honestly said that we sell merchandise at cost, and our profit comes from membership fees, which approach 2 percent of sales. That's not much room for error.

Q: It used to be that warehouse clubs were good places to buy toilet paper and paper towels, but not groceries. Now you can buy just about any food item you want. What happened?

Rich: We had a change in business philosophy. Grocery items increase the *frequency* of shopping. Everyone has to eat, and milk lasts only one week. Food appeals to everybody.

Q: **What are your biggest-selling items?**

Rich: It's still toilet paper and paper towels, but low-fat milk, skinless chicken, and breadmakers are always top sellers.

Q: **What are supermarkets doing to compete?**

Rich: Supermarkets have tried to stem the growth of warehouse clubs, but they cannot move the merchandise as efficiently as we can, nor can they generate the volume necessary to support low prices. The "club buster" sales are actually loss leaders for the supermarkets. Their newspaper ads may feature these items, but they hope you don't buy them.

Remember: The average markup on supermarket items is between 22 and 28 percent. Our limited selection increases efficiency. You won't find twenty-two different brands of peanut butter or forty different kinds of cookies at a warehouse club. But we have to make each item on the floor count. We operate by the "Six Rights of Merchandising." Simply put, that means we have to have the *right merchandise* at the *right time* in the *right place* in the *right quantity* in the *right condition* at the *right price*.

The right merchandise includes new and exciting products. We have to sell what the members want, which generally means name brands, but we're starting to see buyers flock to our private labels.

Q: **What do you mean by that?**

Rich: At Costco, we started the private-label revolution by selling our own club brand, called Kirkland. Since then, private-label goods have grown significantly in market share. That's why you see supermarkets pushing their own store brands. Some commodities such as laundry detergent and soda pop are easily "knocked off," and smart shoppers recognize there isn't much difference in quality.

Private brands cut out the middlemen with all the brokering and advertising costs, plus, private labels make it much more difficult for consumers to comparison shop when the item is not available elsewhere.

Q: **Is that why it's difficult to comparison shop electronic equipment, such as TVs and VCR players, because the model numbers never match up?**

Rich: Exactly. Many name-brand manufacturers create special versions for warehouse clubs—and electronic stores like Circuit City—with different model numbers or face plates. How can a customer compare a Costco Sony Triniton TV, which may have an extra feature on it, against a Sony over at Wal-Mart?

One way to get around this barrier is to go to the library and look up the product in the current *Consumer Reports Buying Guide*. At the end of each section, you'll find a listing of equivalent model numbers. You can also do an Internet search.

Q: **I've noticed that warehouse clubs carry high-quality merchandise and name brands but have a limited selection. What's the reasoning behind that?**

Rich: Limited selection increases efficiency. With fewer vendors to order from and fewer items to stock, fewer mistakes are made. Errors cost money. It is also easier to maintain a limited selection. Can you imagine what life is like for the "re-order" specialist at Home Depot? "Let's see, we have one thousand and one bolts, one thousand and two ..."

In fact, I think limited selection is the primary strength of warehouse clubs. Let's say you walk into a Best Buy or a Circuit City with their walls of televisions, all playing the same Disney video. Where do you begin to shop? How do you know that one television is better than another? I'd rather let the warehouse-club buyer make the decision for me than the sharkskin-suited salesman feeding off commission. That's why we offer excellent products in three price ranges: low-end, mid-range, and high-end.

Limited selection makes shopping easier and clearer for the customer because we often bring in items recommended by *Consumer Reports* magazine, although we can't advertise that fact. But we know our customers tend to read such publications.

Q: **Sometimes I'll see some really off-the-wall goods, like Gucci handbags and Swatches. Where do warehouse clubs get those?**

Rich: We sometimes purchase goods "unconventionally" on the gray market. For example, Levi Strauss may not want to sell to a warehouse club because that would upset The Gap, The Limited, and Miller's Outpost. But then one of those traditional retailers will approach us with an overstocked item, or someone in the distribution chain will divert those goods to us. We have to authenticate the merchandise, of course, because there are counterfeits out there! If we sold fake Seiko watches, for instance, we would lose a tremendous amount of goodwill.

Sometimes, buying unconventionally involves cloak-and-dagger maneuvers. Once, a local tire store was selling Michelins for less than our wholesale prices. We sent a truck over—unmarked—and bought as many tires as we could. When our truck left, their manager tailed our truck to see where it was going. Our people knew they were being followed and made sure they lost him before delivering the tires to our distribution center. It really gets wild out there.

So there you have it, folks, a little peek into the world of warehouse clubs. Before you go out and purchase a membership, however, you have to understand the strengths and weaknesses of warehouse clubs.

THE UPSIDE

- Warehouse clubs have the lowest prices 90 percent of the time. I've done price comparisons on groceries, and warehouse clubs are generally 33–48 percent cheaper.
- Warehouse clubs are starting to sell in smaller bulk sizes. It used to be that you had to buy a ten-gallon drum of tomato sauce or a ten-pound block of jack cheese to get the discount. No longer.
- If you're a name-brand shopper, warehouse clubs are 40–70 percent cheaper than supermarkets' name brands.
- Warehouse clubs' philosophy of limited selection means they can't afford to stock losers.
- Tires, especially high-quality Michelins, will usually be the best deal in town, and mounting costs are very reasonable.
- It's easier to become a warehouse club member than it was ten or fifteen years ago. Basically, you need to be breathing and have $25 in your pocket.

THE DOWNSIDE

- Warehouse clubs don't work for small families or singles. Where are you going to put those forty-eight rolls of toilet paper—under the bed?
- Many warehouse clubs are not conveniently located.
- They don't call warehouse clubs the "$200 Club" for nothing. You have to spend more up front to get your savings.
- There's a real tendency to think, *The more I spend, the more I save.* Warehouse clubs are hoping that you'll come in to get some milk and OJ and drop a $1,999 Mitsubishi big-screen TV in your cart. So what if that big-screen is $500 cheaper? It's still two thousand bucks!

LESSON OF THE DAY

If a warehouse club is within a reasonable distance from your home, buy in bulk as much as you can. Then shop at the super-markets once a week for fresh vegetables and items you can't purchase at a ware-house club. Doing so will give you the best of both shopping worlds.

Cooking Up a Storm

Saving money starts in the kitchen

This is the saddest chapter for me to write because in one generation we have lost the ability—and desire—to cook.

I can't think of the number of times my children, Andrea and Patrick, have returned from a sleepover and told us what they were served for dinner.

They've been fed everything from warmed-up frozen dinners to cold cereal to take-out pizza. Whatever happened to a hearty home-cooked meal with everyone around the table?

Dining is more than eating fresh, nutritious food. When frozen dinners are cooked in the microwave, you can't eat together—or converse—since one meal is being served hot while the other is taking seven minutes to heat up. The communal please-pass-the-corn talk has become as old-fashioned as a Norman Rockwell painting on a *Saturday Evening Post* magazine.

Call me traditional, call me a solitary voice in the wilderness, or call me cheap, but eating a "regular" dinner all together is the best investment you can make in your family—relationally *and* financially.

The dinner hour is often the only time a family sees each other the entire day. *But you don't know our schedules. We've got Boy Scouts and youth group and Little League and piano lessons.*

So do we. We've eaten many a meal at 7:30 on weeknights so that all of us could sit and sup together. *But we never have anything in the fridge. And it takes too much time and effort to get something on the dinner table. I'm tired at the end of the day.*

Listen: A little time and a little effort will save you, oh, $25 to $40 a pop when you compare the cost of eating out to the cost of eating in. Multiply that by two, three times a week, and we're talking some significant savings—$400 a month. You should be looking at your kitchen as a profit center.

Let's say you're a family of four, and your oldest son's soccer game just finished. It's 7:15, the kids are delirious with hunger, and you're driving home. It would be tempting to swing into Chili's and scarf down a quick order of mushroom burgers, fries, and lemonades, but this little diversion will cost you at least $35 (or a few dollars less if you have small children who order kid's meals).

Even if you stop at Boston Market for a takeout dinner (called an HMR, or "home meal replacement," in the restaurant business), it's going to set you back at least $5 a head. Instead, stay the course and go home for a meal of good leftovers.

Before you groan, hear me out. When Nicole cooks, she always makes enough so that we can get at least one meal of leftovers. I'm talking about mouth-watering entrees such as cut-up chicken breasts cooked in white-cream-and-mushroom sauce, pasta primavera with rich seafood, homemade egg rolls, and even homemade pizza (our bread machine makes the dough, and pizza can be healthy when covered with low-fat toppings).

This "thrice-a-week" cooking works for us, but there's more than one way to skin a chicken breast. I've come across three cooking systems that offer detailed, step-by-step plans for daily meal preparation. These cooking systems—called once-a-month cooking, mega-cooking, and 15-minute cooking—concentrate your preparation time into blocks, saving precious minutes and even hours in your day, and get you out of the habit of serving expensive convenience foods such as Lean Cuisine. (Did you know that serving four of those tiny nine-ounce Chicken Piccata dinners will cost your family $11.96? And if you have a teenager experiencing a growth spurt, he can chow down three of those babies.)

You can decide which, if any, of these cooking systems will work in your household, or you can go with Nicole's "thrice-a-week" cooking. But pick one, because you'll save a lot of money by staying out of restaurants.

ONCE-A-MONTH COOKING

Mimi Wilson, who wrote the book *Once-a-Month Cooking* with Mary Beth Lagerborg, says, "I developed this plan because I felt I had to do something drastic to squeeze more time into my day. I had three young children, a busy husband, and guests at our home two or three times a week. I used time studies to see where I wasted the most minutes, and I found it was in making meals from scratch every day." Mimi also wanted to reduce food waste and have a ministry of spontaneous hospitality.

Once-a-month cooking enabled Mimi to reach her goals by cooking a month's (or two weeks') worth of dinner entrees in a single day, then freezing them.

The first step in implementing their system, say Mimi and Mary Beth, is to choose a menu from their book. Family chefs have several choices, including low-fat fare, company dishes, and plenty of good "kid food." Then it's off to the supermarket with a detailed shopping list. The next day is a cooking marathon—all day and perhaps into the evening for a month's worth of entrees and about six hours for two weeks' worth of good eating. But, as Mary Beth points out, "When it's done, it's *done."* All thirty entrees, some packaged in plastic bags, will fit into a refrigerator freezer when the preparation is complete.

The *Once-a-Month Cooking* book does all the planning for you, outlining exactly what dishes to prepare and when. Mary Beth and Mimi also detail tips for shopping, cooking, freezing, saving money, and adapting the system to your own recipes. In addition to recipes for entrees, there is also a chapter of "More Recipes to Enhance Meals."

MEGA-COOKING

Jill Bond wrote down her mega-cooking system when friends asked how she managed her time. "They wanted to know how I could get everything done around the home," explains Jill, "and still have time to write, do crafts, home school my children, volunteer in my church and community, and manage a home-based business. I have about ten more hours in my week through mega-cooking."

Jill prepares six months' worth of entrees at one time. You heard me right—*six months.* She, her husband, Alan, and some of their four children work together for most of a weekend, preparing about 180 entrees. They cook huge batches of chili, sweet-and-sour meatballs, chicken entrees, and thirty to forty other kinds of dishes—all divided into dinner-size servings and frozen for later use. This system differs from once-a-month cooking in that many batches of the same dish are all prepared at one time. Her book, *Dinner's in the Freezer,* has recipes and shows you how to do it.

Mega-cooking, especially when preparing nearly 200 meals, can seem overwhelming for the beginner. She suggests you start small, perhaps with something as simple as tripling tonight's lasagna recipe and freezing two portions.

15-MINUTE COOKING

Rhonda Barfield's 15-minute cooking system breaks food preparation time into two short, daily sessions. The evening meal is started in the morning (or the night before), then finished right before dinner. Quantities are large to allow for some leftovers for breakfast and/or lunch the next day. Once a week a "leftovers meal" (soup, casserole, and so forth) is prepared, so little food is wasted. Daily menus and game plans feature "Tips for Healthier Eating" and "Tips to Save More Money."

Rhonda's book *15-Minute Cooking* presents twenty-eight days of menus (including a daily entree, bread, vegetables and/or salad and dessert), detailed game plans to tell you how to do what and when, and shopping lists.

Which system would work best for you? Place yourself in the following questions and answers:

Q: **How do you prefer to manage your time? Would you rather cook in small segments daily or in one large block?** If you answered, "small segments," 15-minute cooking might work best for you. You could also mega-cook a single meal each night for, say, a week: triple the entree recipe and freeze two servings. A compromise would be to use *Once-a-Month Cooking*'s Two-Week Entree Plan.

If you prefer meal preparation in large blocks, once-a-month cooking or mega-cooking are better choices for you.

Q: **How important is saving money?** All three cooking systems save money. If you're buying twenty pounds of ground beef, for example, you can negotiate with the store butcher and probably get a discount. Canned veggies and tomato sauce purchased in extra-large cans at a warehouse club are incredibly cheap, and you can buy fresh produce in quantity discounts at a farmer's market.

Q: Are you concerned about eating healthy foods?

Once-a-Month Cooking specifically outlines a Low-Fat Entree Plan for fifteen days. *Dinner's in the Freezer* makes suggestions for lower-fat cooking and sugar substitutes. *15-Minute Cooking* includes daily "Tips for Healthier Eating."

Q: How do you get these books?

- *Dinner's in the Freezer* by Jill Bond is available in Christian bookstores nationwide, or by calling the publisher, Great Christian Books, at (800) 775–5422 to order.

- *Once-a-Month Cooking* by Mimi Wilson and Mary Beth Lagerborg is available in both Christian and secular bookstores nationwide. Or call Focus on the Family, (800) 232–6459, to request a copy.

- *15-Minute Cooking* by Rhonda Barfield is available by calling Great Christian Books (800) 775–5422, or by ordering directly from the Barfields at Lilac Publishing, P.O. Box 665, St. Charles, MO 63302. An eight-page catalog explaining the 15-minute cooking system is free to all who write or e-mail at barfield@aol.com.

Q: Which system is best for me?

Actually, the final choice is up to you. The next time you're dreading the dinner hour, resolve to give one of these cooking systems a try. You and your children will be glad you did, and maybe your waistline will, too!

━━━━━━━━━━━━━━━━━━━━━━ LESSON OF THE DAY

Anytime you chop, slice, carve, dice, blend, peel, crush, sauté, spice, shake, bake, broil, barbecue, or baste your own food, you're saving tons over eating out.

Eating Out

You can cut your restaurant bill as easily as saying "We'll drink water"

The next time you walk out of Cracker Barrel and ask yourself, *Did I really pay $45 for four meat loaf and chicken finger meals?,* consider the plight of Arie and Lynn Van Wingerden.

The Van Wingerdens have twenty-two children, and this isn't a typographical error. When Arie and Lynn decide to take the family out, they better find a deal, or otherwise it'll cost them a nice car payment. The Van Wingerdens like to frequent Country Buffet, an all-you-can-eat cafeteria.

"We've found that Country Buffet is cheaper than even McDonald's because they offer a 'pay by the age' setup for the kids," Lynn says. "They charge fifty cents per year up to age eleven, so our usual bill is $115 to $120. Of course, that's assuming my husband gets the bus driver's discount," she adds with a laugh.

I wouldn't know whether to laugh or cry—having to fork over $120 every time I took the family out to eat—but when you're a family of twenty-four, you play all the angles.

YOU CAN LOOK IT UP

If we're a nation that has forgotten how to cook, then we've become a nation that loves to be served in restaurants. We eat in restaurants an average of 4.1 times per week, according to the National Restaurant Association, or 213 restaurant meals a year. If you attach a dollar figure—let's call it $6 a meal—then you're spending $1,278 a year *per person!* Multiply that by four for a typical family, and the figure approaches $5,000 annually. (Let's not even think what it would cost the Van Wingerdens. Oops, I did: $30,672!)

Yes, it's nice to be served, chow down on some tasty food, and have someone else do the clean-up, but we pay dearly for the convenience. Lest you think that I'm a fuddy-duddy, I love to eat out as much as the next person. The problem is that we've forgotten to make eating out an *occasion.* Sitting down in a restaurant should be a time of unhurried conversation, a period of family interaction, a respite from the daily routine. Instead it's a quickly served mesquite chicken breast, soggy fries, and a flat Coke amidst a raucous atmosphere in which you are expected to "turn over" your table in one hour.

Whatever happened to telling the family, "You know, we haven't been in a restaurant in weeks. Where shall we go out this weekend?"

Then you've made eating out a family event, something to be eagerly anticipated. You can discuss which restaurant to go to; I prefer "mom and pop" family-owned establishments with atmosphere. I'll never forget the Mexican restaurant in the bad part of town when we lived east of Los Angeles. The well-lit parking lot with a rent-a-cop watching your car certainly made for some "atmosphere."

Besides, there are way too many "concept" and chain restaurants such as Chevys, American Pasta Co., Eastside Marios, Chilis, Chi-Chi's, and Acapulcos sprouting up like spring mushrooms. I remember traveling to Nashville with Nicole to interview Christian singer Steve Green. The plan was to go out for dinner with Steve and his wife, Marijean. As we turned into the mall parking lot, Steve steered the car toward a busy Macaroni Grill.

The day before, Nicole and I had just eaten at Macaroni Grill in Colorado Springs. The Nashville version was exactly the same, right down to the Italian language lessons piped into the restrooms!

STRATEGIES FOR SIT-DOWN RESTAURANTS

- **Eat out less often—it's as simple as that.** If you're looking for another rationale for staying home, remind yourself that you can eat *better* at home. You can purchase a lot of pork tenderloin or even Alaskan king crab for the price of a simple meal at Applebee's Neighborhood Grill & Bar.
- **Know that it's going to cost you more than you think.** Let's say that you and your spouse have a date night at T.G.I.Friday's. You go easy, passing on appetizers and ordering two blackened Cajun chicken meals, priced at $7.59. Mentally, you're figuring $16, maybe a couple of dollars more with tip.

   Actually, your two meals will set you back more than $30. Beneath the description for the Cajun chicken, the fine print said you could order a house salad for an extra $1.89. *That doesn't seem like much to get some greens.* Then you ordered two ice teas at $1.49 each. Although your waitress did her best to entice you with the dessert tray, you stood firm, but you ordered coffee to round out the meal ($1.49 each).

The cost of the two meals, when you add 6 percent sales tax and a 15 percent tip, comes to $30.42. And you haven't even included the five or ten bucks for a baby-sitter.

• **Brown-bag your lunch at work.** I have to admit to a twinge of jealousy when I see coworkers eat out every single weekday, but bringing my own lunch to work saves me $6 a day or $120 a month. I'd rather spend that money on the family than on myself.

• **Sign up for dining clubs.** Every major city has them— entertainment books or dining clubs that cost $20 to $35 for a one-year membership. What you get is a card that allows you two-for-one dining at participating restaurants. For me, the discount has to be at least 50 percent on the entrees, because it's not 50 percent off the meal—just the entrees. You add appetizers, salad, dessert, and drinks at full price.

• **Speaking of add-ons—watch the add-ons.** You should eat at restaurants that serve complete meals—entrees served with bread and salad or soup. Appetizers and desserts can turn a $25 check for two into a $50 check quicker than you can say "shrimp cocktail" and "tiramisu." Besides, you can eat dessert at home.

• **Drink water.** Most restaurants charge at least a buck for a soft drink or lemonade, so for a family of four, drinks will cost you $5 with tax and tip. Drinking water may take some getting used to ("Dad, it's not a 'treat' unless we have Coke"), but remind the family that water is much healthier than high-calorie soft drinks. Also, can you do without the dessert coffee? That can add another 10 percent to the bill.

• **Go out for lunch instead of dinner.** Many restaurants serve the same menu for lunch and dinner. You just have to pay 25 percent more for the privilege of eating after 4:00 P.M.

- **Look for coupon and "early-bird" specials.** Saturday is the most popular day to eat out, followed by Friday and Sunday. Restaurants are not willing to discount these high-peak times. But newspaper or junk-mail coupons can be found for other weekdays or early-bird specials before 6:00 P.M.
- **Know that restaurants in vacation areas heavily advertise their early-bird specials as a way to spread out the "rush."** This is how we like to vacation: sleep until 9:00 A.M., have a big brunch, snack on a piece of fruit in the afternoon, and be hungry to eat at five o'clock, when the early birds start.
- **If you have two or more teenage boys in the house, get to know your Country Buffets and smorgasbords.** When I was fourteen and in my growth spurt, I can remember eating three pork chops and mounds of mashed potatoes at one sitting. Country Buffets can handle ravenous teens. One final tip: The food tastes better when you take the tray away. That's an old college dorm trick.

STRATEGIES FOR FAST FOOD

- **Skip the supersize.** Not only are the restaurants padding their profits, they're padding your digestive system with significantly higher fat and calorie counts.
- **Drink water.** This advice works great in fast-food restaurants, too. And ordering a la carte *sans* soft drink is cheaper than ordering a "value meal."
- **Pass on the happy meals.** This is an all-time "gotcha," because who can refuse the pleading eyes of your four-year-old daughter who *has* to have the latest Disney toy?

You're paying a lot for a figurine that'll get tossed under the bed the next day.

- **If you drive the kids to Wendy's for a "treat," you don't have to eat.** Just sit in the booth and talk with them.
- **If you're traveling to an out-of-town soccer game, pack a lunch for along the way.** Where is it written that a family must worship at the altar of McDonald's anytime it drives an hour from home? A cooler filled with sandwiches, rice cakes, chips, trail mixes, string cheese, fruit, and granola bars should make the kids happy.
- **If you're traveling long distances, get off the main drag.** Along the South Carolina coast a couple of years ago, we followed the back streets to a sandwich shop backing up to a coastal inlet. No one told us that a crocodile was going to be swimming off the back porch!
- **If you are going to make a fast-food stop, my vote is Taco Bell.** You can eat four tacos for around $2.60 a person (with water), and get some lettuce, tomato, and cheese in your tacos.

LESSON OF THE DAY

Reserve restaurants for an occasion,
and you'll do just fine.

Clothes Shopping

When to buy, when to wait, where to go

What if they gave a clothes sale and nobody came?

Every time you open a newspaper or stroll down a mall, some clothing store has a sale going on. One "Moonlight Madness" sale may draw hordes of frenzied customers from the hinterlands, while another "End-of-Season" promotion induces yawns from windowshoppers.

Still, it helps to understand the cyclical nature of this volatile business, since today's fashion statement is often tomorrow's featured "doorbuster." First and foremost, clothes are as perishable an item as iceberg lettuce. Major department stores and mall clothing emporiums give slacks, sweaters, tank tops, polo shirts, pants, and shorts a three-month sales window—and then they're relegated to the clearance racks.

Those racks are tucked away in the back because stores don't want to give the appearance that the whole floor is on sale. The clearance racks are where clothes go for their first markdown—usually 25–30 percent.

Since this is the first discount, you can often find your size at these racks. The next markdown—to 50 percent—is usually held during once-a-quarter "Seasonal Clearance" sales, but be careful: there's a good chance the popular sizes will be gone. You can gamble and wait for your size to be there at the half-off sale, but most clothes on the final markdown rack are women's size 3–5 or men's 36–38.

You should also know that clothes are sold in advance of the "season," which means winter jackets are set out in September, sweaters and Christmas apparel in October, bermuda shorts in March, summer skirts in April, beachwear in May, and back-to-school clothes in July. If you can anticipate your clothing needs—let's say your middle-school boy will need a new winter coat next fall—then you can make a great deal by buying in February.

When you sort through the clearance racks, try to decipher the price tags. The exercise can be fun, so here's how it works: All clothes are labeled with a code indicating when the item hit the floor. The upper-left corner of a sales ticket may read 8947, which means the item was set out in 1998 (the store reversed the last two digits of the year) in the fourth week of the seventh month (July). Other stores may put a number between 1 and 52, denoting which week of the year the item came in.

If you chat up a bored salesperson, he or she will often tell you how to read the code, which can be put to your advantage. An example would be when you find that perfect Nautica golf tie for Father's Day. Looking at the tag you notice that it came in last November—probably as a Christmas gift item. Present the tie to a manager (the only ones authorized to make markdowns) and say, "Excuse me, but I notice that this tie has been around since Christmas. Is it possible it didn't make it to the sales rack?" More often than not, you'll get the discount.

You should also present flaws in the clothes—a missing button, a hem that needs to be stitched, or a dirty smudge—to the manager. Again, say that you are willing to buy that item, but is there a discount?

To help you sort through the clothes shopping maze, I'm going to break it down into several categories.

THE DEPARTMENT STORES

At the top of the food chain are the department stores. They have the largest ad budgets, the greatest selection, and the most willingness to let clothes go for pennies on the dollar.

Aba Arthur, who studied fashion design in London, works at Joslin's in Colorado Springs as a "personal shopper." She assists people who don't have time to shop or don't know what to buy, and advises those who want to redo their wardrobe.

Upscale department stores like Joslin's, Dayton-Hudson, May Co., and Nordstrom can be excellent places to scoop up bargains, but you have to be willing to wait for their major sales, which happen two, three times a year. (Look for them in October and a month or two *after* Christmas.)

These highly advertised sales often discount high-end goods by 50 percent and, depending on the chain, run ten-minute "doorbusters" in which the clothes are wheeled out on Z-racks to the waiting mob. I've seen $200 Liz Claiborne dresses go for $9.99. That's what I mean when I say that large department stores want it *out of there*.

It's easy to get caught up in the feeding frenzy of these stupendous sales, so watch the impulse items. The sales always begin on Friday morning, but pricing is usually completed by Thursday afternoon, so drop in early Thursday evening and get a jump on everyone else. "If you come on Thursday and the signs are up, we honor the prices," said Aba.

When I asked Aba for shopping tips, she stressed quality. "If you buy quality, you can have an item for a long time," she said. "Look for brand names like Austin Reed, Dana Buchman, and Geoffrey Beene. And get to know personal shoppers like me. Let us know who you are. Just the other day, I pulled two women's suits for a good customer of mine because they went on sale. I'm holding them for her in the back right now."

Aba also said she sees shoppers who hold up an item and say, "I can sew this."

"I used to sew quite a bit," said Aba, "but fabric is so expensive now. I'm afraid it's cheaper to buy something on sale than it is to make it."

THE BIG RETAILERS

If your town has more than two stoplights, there's a good chance you have a Sears, JCPenney, or Montgomery Ward close by. These stores do not have splashy sales on clothes, although JCPenney's Red Tag specials are worth checking out.

Sid Mashburn, who owns a Christian clothing firm called Three Trees, believes JCPenney is the best store in the country for buying clothes. "JCPenney has a huge private-label program, and they are very close to where the leading fashion people are, but never in a weird way. They don't do trendy stuff. Instead, they stick with classic, straight-ahead clothes in good colors and good quality. They also sell the best T-shirt in America—the JCPenney polo T-shirt."

THE SPECIALTY RETAILERS

If you (or more likely, your teenager) just *gotta* have fashion, then step inside The Gap, Banana Republic, Old Navy, Abercrombie & Fitch, Talbot's, or Eddie Bauer.

"These stores are well-priced and no-nonsensical in their approach," said Sid. "They deal in fashion basics, but their most fashionable things are never too trendy. The Gap tends to take their mark-downs very quickly. They deliver into the store about seven times a year, or about once every six weeks. They start marking down items in the fourth or fifth week. [Author's note: Remember what I said about reading sales tags?] But I don't care who you are, you can always find great stuff on the sales racks at The Gap."

Best buys in these stores are blue jeans and khaki pants, since they are often "loss leaders" to bring teens (and their parents) into the store. Store-wide sales are infrequent, however, and markdowns rarely get past 25 percent.

THE DISCOUNTERS

With a Wal-Mart in every burg, it's no wonder they are the nation's Number 1 retailer. You'll also find Kmart and Target in this category.

What can I say that you don't already know? Kmart's "Blue Light Specials" are lampooned in Jay Leno monologues, and we all know to "watch for falling prices" at Wal-Mart. In our house, we joke about shopping at "Tarzhay."

All kidding aside, these retailers' financial muscle allows them to buy in huge quantities, and they work off a relatively small mark-up. These stores are good when you can't wait for a sale on boys' shorts that you needed yesterday. Socks, underwear, and bras are fairly priced.

THE OFF-PRICERS

Since they don't advertise, you never know what you'll find on the sale racks at T.J. Maxx, Marshall's, Filene's Basement, and

Ross Dress for Less, which is part of the charm of shopping these chains. They *want* you to drop by and see what bargains they have.

Sid Mashburn says you have to watch out for irregulars with these discounters. "An irregular is something they've labeled as medium but it's actually a large," said Sid. "Or there's a tear under the sleeve or a misweave in the fabric. Also, watch for discoloration."

FACTORY STORES

Located outside of major metropolitan areas or near resort areas, factory outlets have sprung up around the country like mushrooms following a spring storm. More than 300 dot the landscape from Portland, Oregon, to Portland, Maine.

Discounts are so-so. You're never going to get a *great* deal at a Laura Ashley or Nike outlet store. You might be able to knock 20 percent off a pair of Air Jordans.

But hey, you're on vacation with the family, and you see this oasis of shopping on the horizon . . .

WAREHOUSE CLUBS

The selection is very limited and you can't try on slacks or pants, but warehouse clubs are incredible. I've seen nice leather tennis shoes at Costco for $19.95, and leather jackets are half the going rate.

Don't laugh, but warehouse clubs may be the best deal of all.

LESSON OF THE DAY

You should never have to pay retail for clothes because the competition is insane.

DAY 8

Big-Ticket Appliances

Refrigerator died? Need a new TV?

During a summer heat wave a couple of years ago, our refrigerator couldn't get cooler than forty degrees. Milk lasted a day or two before it turned sour. Leftovers had to be eaten fast. Lettuce went limp.

This was the third summer that our fifteen-year-old fridge couldn't beat the heat. We had vacuumed the coils and called in Bud's Appliance in previous years, but this time the fridge didn't respond. With Nicole's brother and his family of five flying in for a month-long visit, something had to be done. In a hurry.

I understand that you're supposed to "shop" the big-ticket items, but time was not on our side. I immediately rifled through the classified ads, but laying down money on a ten-year-old fridge didn't make sense. We looked at a six-year-old Kenmore for $600, but that plain-Jane model didn't even have an ice maker.

So we decided to buy new.

A decent refrigerator—with side-by-side doors and water and ice in the door—will cost you more than $1,000. One reason new refrigerators cost so much is that new federal regulations that went into effect in 1995 mandated that refrigerators be made without chlorofluorocarbons, which damage the earth's ozone layer.

We had to educate ourselves and find the best deal pronto. The schooling came from a back issue of *Consumer Reports* that rated various refrigerators. Then Nicole made the rounds of the major appliance dealers: Sears, Montgomery Ward, Best Buy, even Sam's Warehouse. She also sought scratch-and-dent models and close-outs.

After she narrowed down our options, we settled on a sale-priced Amana at Montgomery Ward.

I think we did as well as could be expected, but I learned something: when a major appliance breaks, few of us have the luxury of leisurely shopping for a new one. "People are in a tight window and are driven by need when they walk into our store," one sales manager told me. "People tend to push appliances to their limit."

I can raise my hand to that. For years we coaxed a fifteen-year-old washing machine that constantly went out of whack on the spin cycle. But when she started smoking and leaking oil recently, we *knew* the machine was not repairable.

Again, we read our *Consumer Reports* and paced the aisles of major appliance stores. We settled on a close-out Amana.

Spot a trend here? *Customer's appliance dies. Needs one in a hurry. Reads* Consumer Reports *to "educate" himself. Shops the big appliance stores. Picks a close-out model.*

We did as well as could be expected. When I talked to Judith Pritchard at Best Buy (where we bought our new washing machine), she told me that they know informed shoppers read *Consumer Reports.*

That's why Best Buy and other appliance outlets will attach a white cardboard saying, "Ranked Number 1 by a leading consumer magazine." *Consumer Reports* does not allow its name to be used in advertisements, but informed shoppers know whom they're talking about. The top-rated appliances have the fewest repairs and highest customer satisfaction.

"Do *Consumer Reports* ratings generally jive with what you know?" I asked Judith.

"Most definitely," she replied.

Appliances are sold in three levels. First, there is the "advertised piece"—the $299 washer we see bannered in the store's newspaper ad. The attractive price drives us into the store, but after looking around and talking with the salesperson, we quickly learn that for $50 or $75 more, we can purchase the "step piece," the washer with some it-would-be-nice-to-have features—like a warm wash/warm rinse cycle. The third level is the "high-end piece" with bells and whistles that we can live without, such as computerized readouts and six spin cycles.

Most of us purchase the "step piece," which is okay. The major retailers generally put a couple of appliances on sale every three weeks, which they advertise in Sunday newspaper inserts. This way, they always have something "on sale," although it's only one or two refrigerators, one or two washers, one or two dryers.... Discounts are modest—around 7–10 percent. A couple of times a year, however, appliance stores will have an EOS—"Everything On Sale."

Your best bet for a discount is close-out sales on year-end models, usually held in June, when the new model year begins. Appliance sales is a competitive business with low mark-ups of around 20 percent, so don't expect deep discounts. The new refrigerator and washer we purchased were year-end closeouts, which saved us $200 and $75, respectively.

WHERE SHOULD YOU BUY?

Appliances have become another "killer-category" segment, with Best Buy and Circuit City competing against the Searses and Montgomery Wards of the retail world. Even Home Depot is getting into the act; I saw washing machines at my local store. But don't forget the "independents"—family-owned stores that have been around for years. They know what the big boys charge for their Maytag washers, and they also know that they have to be competitive if they want to keep their doors open. The independents usually have experienced salespeople—many with ten, twenty years in the business—where the other stores will have "fast floor" salespeople who memorize four or five key points about the appliance.

Wherever you end up, be listening for the "trial close." That's when the salesperson tries to close the sale by saying something like, "If I have that color, can I deliver it to you tomorrow?" He's asking for the sale. Stand your ground and reply that you haven't made up your mind yet.

Here are a few other things to keep in mind:

- *Value* **should be your goal.** One appliance store owner told me that customers walk into his store thinking price, but by the time they plunk down their money, price has dropped way down the list—underneath features, manufacturer's reputation, and size of the appliance. Perhaps that's the way it should be when you're shopping for an appliance you plan on keeping for ten or more years.

- **Be willing to set your sights lower.** What happens if you can't afford a thousand bucks for a new refrigerator but don't want to buy used from the classifieds? Then set your sights on a $500 new refrigerator. Sure, it won't have flowing ice and cold water in the door or fancy egg holders, but it will keep your food and drinks cold. The other option is to look at stores that sell refurbished appliances, which come with some sort of guarantee.

- **Keep an eye on front-loading washers.** Re-introduced in 1997, front-loading washers are too expensive to recommend (they generally run $799), but when they get cheaper, they'll give top-loading washers a spin for their money. Reason: front-loading washers sip hot water, using half as much as top-loading washers. So what if you have to bend over? You will certainly enjoy writing a smaller check for your utilities.

- **Go for the 27-inch TVs.** I know this chapter has dwelt on "white goods" (kitchen and household appliances), but I did want to say something about "black goods"—television sets. The hot thing these days is home theater set-ups, for which you can pay thousands of dollars for Surround Sound and huge sixty-inch "projection" screens.

  While I like to watch television, I don't want me or my family to watch *too much* TV. Thus, I see no reason to spend thousands on the latest technology to watch programs and sitcoms that go totally against my Christian worldview.

  The prices for 27-inch TVs, which have a plenty large screen, have dropped dramatically in the last couple of years. You should be able to bring home a nice 27-inch TV for under $500. This should do until HDTV (high-definition television) changes the face of television, but we're five to ten years from that development.

- **Watch for the aftersell.** After you've swallowed hard and purchased that $1,700 GE Profile refrigerator, brace yourself for the extended warranty pitch.

When weighing this form of insurance, know that you're basically covered for one year by the manufacturer. Then ask yourself these four questions:

1. If the item breaks, can I afford the loss?
2. Am I getting my money's worth?
3. What exactly does the policy cover?
4. Is the coverage necessary?

Looked at another way, insurance companies are profit-driven like any other company. Really, what are the odds of your fridge breaking during the life of the extended warranty? Also keep in mind that extended warranties will often duplicate existing manufacturer coverage.

"You shouldn't buy insurance on appliances," said Glenn Daily, a New York fee-only insurance consultant. "The payout is traditionally very low. That's probably one of the worst deals in insurance."

A possible exception: Best Buy's Four-Year Performance Plan, which costs $59 for four years. Fifteen dollars a year is not bad, especially for an expensive refrigerator!

I did hear a horror story, however. One appliance salesperson told me he heard of an elderly woman who purchased a 13-inch color TV for $130, then opted for an $80 extended warranty. Now that doesn't make sense.

LESSON OF THE DAY

It's Murphy's Law that appliances die at the most inopportune times. Educate yourself, shop the "step pieces," and make sure the extended warranties are worth it.

Buying It Used

How to shop garage sales and classified ads for the best deal

I grew up in a home in which Saturday mornings revolved around "garage saling." I learned to love the thrill of a good find, and all through childhood I was outfitted in jackets, shirts, and pants bought at garage sales. I never thought twice about wearing "used clothes."

In 1970, while I was in high school, I came across my greatest buy—a box of old *Chicago Tribune* newspapers headlining cataclysmic events of days past:

- November 11, 1917, the Day World War I—"The War To End All Wars"—Ended in Europe.
- May 22, 1927, the Day After Charles Lindbergh Landed in Paris, the First Man To Fly the Atlantic Ocean Nonstop.
- September 2, 1939, the Day After Germany Invaded Poland.
- December 8, 1941, the Day After the Sneak Attack on Pearl Harbor By the Japanese.

I paid $3 for nearly three dozen historic newspapers (which I store in my office for safekeeping), but I fear the proverbial bloom is off the garage-saling rose. I don't know how garage sales are in your hometown, but it's not like the good old days. Here in Colorado, it's slim pickings even during the garage sale "season," which runs from late spring to Labor Day.

When I called my mom, Anne Yorkey, in San Diego, I asked if she felt the same. She wholeheartedly agreed. "I rarely bother any more," she said. "The dishes are chipped, the clothes have spots and a woolen smell of mildew, and the furniture is broken. I see stuff I would hesitate to give to St. Vincent de Paul, let alone try to sell," said Mom.

If something raises my mother's interest, it's usually over-priced. "The prices I see these days are incredible. People think their cherished items are worth a lot more than they really are."

Still, I'm not going to give up on garage sales. I've had some good days in past years, like the time I found a pair of eight-feet long, eight-feet-high wooden shelves that had been nailed together with set screws. Perfect for my garage, the shelves cost $20 each. The lumber had to cost four times that amount!

But there's another reason I like to go to garage sales: it's cheap entertainment for the family, spending an hour sifting through other people's junk.

If you're going to be successful at garage sales, this is what you should do:

1. **Know your terms:**
   - "Garage sale" means *we're selling the junk that's been in the kids' closets for ages.*
   - "Moving sale" means *we're moving to another home, and we don't want to lug our junk there. If you don't buy it, it's going to Goodwill.* You'll find more furniture, garden tools, book collections, and better prices at moving sales.
   - "Estate sale" means *someone died in the family and we're selling off the effects* or *we're getting on in years and it's time*

to downsize. There's a lot of old stuff here, and it means a lot to us, so don't expect a good deal. Estate sales are not held in garages but inside homes, and they are often run by estate-sale specialists who get a cut of the action. You usually have to take a number and wait outside the home since those staging the sale want to keep an eye on light-fingered shoppers. Plus, there really may be some nice stuff inside.

2. Read the paper and use a highlighter to mark the sales you want to visit. Then number them in order so you won't have to backtrack. The newspaper descriptions can't be relied upon: They all say "children's clothes and toys." You just have to take your chances. Sales that pool several families increase your odds of a successful day, however.

Look up addresses on a street map *before* you get in the car. Getting lost costs you time and makes the experience a drag for everybody. Finally, bring plenty of quarters and dollar bills. Who knows? You might be able to bargain better by having the correct change.

3. Stick to a certain area of town. It's not an efficient use of time to drive twenty minutes to one sale and then fifteen minutes to another. Also, shop neighborhoods that have kids the same age as yours.

4. Once you've decided where you're going to go, start early. The good stuff is gone after the first hour, so if you're going to make the effort to hit the streets, do so by 8:00 or 8:30 on Saturday morning (unless you live in a part of the country with Friday garage sales). The very *best* time to arrive is fifteen minutes before starting time. Most people are working feverishly to get the stuff in the driveway and mark a few prices. If you find an unpriced item, you might be able to swing a good deal because they are rushed.

5. Know what things are worth. As Mom said, there are some inflated prices these days. T-shirts and school shirts should go for 25 cents; pants for 50 cents. A really nice sweater might be a buck or two. OshKosh overalls, which wear like iron, are worth a few dollars. Soccer shoes, a garage sale favorite, should go for $2 to $5. Toys and games are rarely worth more than 50 cents. Electronic items—GameBoys, cassette players, TVs—should go for pennies on the dollar, since they can't be guaranteed.

6. The best age to buy clothes for your children is when they are under six. Preschoolers don't wear their clothes out, they outgrow them, so anything you find should still be in very good condition.

7. Be a good bargainer. You'd think that most people would just want to get rid of their old clothes and junk, so test that hypothesis. Point out flaws in clothes, then make a low-ball offer. Buy a bunch of stuff that adds up to $5, then offer $4. You'll get it.

You want to pay such a low price because if the item tears or breaks tomorrow, you haven't lost much. Know that you have your best leverage after noontime, when traffic is slow and those holding the sale are looking in the Yellow Pages for a thrift store to come haul their stuff away. You might be able to pick up those unsold items for next to nothing.

8. Ask for items you don't see. Let's say you're on the look-out for an infant car seat. If you don't see one, ask the people holding the sale if they have one put away. They may just decide to let you haul it off for two bucks!

9. Don't overlook thrift stores. You're not going to save money at thrift stores over garage sales, but thrift shops do have more selection. In my hometown, the ARC Thrift Store has a once-a-month "everything's 99 cents" sale. That's a great price for jackets, shoes, and sports coats.

CLASSIFIED ADS

If you're going to shop classified ads for furniture, used appliances, firewood, or musical instruments, draw on your reservoir of patience.

Locally, we have the *Thrifty Nickel*, which contains pages and pages of *unclassified* ad items. Boy, that's a drag to read, since the ad for a 586 computer is next to the one for an upright freezer.

Thankfully, daily newspapers classify their ads, but classified ad shopping is the way to buy big-ticket items that you usually can't find at garage sales.

The same rules apply—you're buying used and have no guarantee, so *caveat emptor*. It will take time to drive around town and "talk up" the sale item with the seller ("Why are you selling it?" "Is there anything I should know?" or "How much does it cost to fix?").

Drive by an ATM machine before arriving so you can have cash on hand. A couple of years ago I bought a new-in-the-box Apple StyleWriter 2400 printer (and I could tell it hadn't been used) for $100 off the mail-order price because I had $275 in my pocket. You bargain better when you pay cash instead of asking the private party to take your check.

I'm also glad to see the trend in used "business" stores: places like Play It Again Sports, Computer Renaissance, and One More Time specialize in used sporting goods, CDs, computers, tools, furniture, and consignment clothes. Revenues at thrift and resale stores have risen 10 percent annually in recent years, while traditional retailers have seen little or no growth.

LESSON OF THE DAY

If you have a special need, pray about it with the family. Watch your children's faith grow—and yours as well—when you pray to find a baseball mitt at a garage sale or a two-year-old refrigerator with ice and water in the door.

DAY 10

Getting Some Wheels

The auto retail market is changing before our eyes

Today we're going to talk about cars, but I know that you're reading it here first.

I have a close friend—let's call him Robert—who owns a Ford dealership in the southeast. When I called to ask him about buying new and used cars, I could sense the concern in his voice.

He told me that the Ford Motor Company had been quietly buying up all the Ford, Lincoln-Mercury, and Jaguar dealerships in Indianapolis, Indiana. "Ford is trying to control all the retail outlets and quick satellite service centers in and around Indianapolis," said Robert.

"Have any of the Detroit auto manufacturers tried to buy dealerships before?"

"No, and that's what concerns me. If they get control of the distribution system they can undersell the middlemen—dealers like me. While that may initially drive the price of cars down, ultimately I don't think the consumer will be served any better. For small businessmen like me, the customer is all we have."

It doesn't sound feasible that the Big Three automakers—Ford, GM, and Chrysler—could buy up dealerships around the country, but "they have the financial muscle to make it happen," said Robert. "This is how they could do it," he explained. "Either I sell now to them for top dollar, or I hold out," he said. "But if Ford buys several dealerships in my territory, they can cut prices so low that my dealership would be worth nothing. So the question is: do I sell high now or hope to stay in business and possibly lose it all later?"

I tell this story not to elicit sympathy for auto dealers—who are doing just fine, thank you—but to lift the window shade on an industry that is undergoing seismic changes this decade. H. Wayne Huizenga, the Florida billionaire who owns Blockbuster video, Waste Management, and the Miami Dolphins, has plans to turn auto retailing into another "killer category" segment. Called Auto-Nation, Huizenga's used-car superstores are taking their place alongside Home Depots, Best Buys, CompUSAs, and PetsMarts.

Huizenga plans to have 100 AutoNations dotting the country with no-haggle pricing, snappy-looking car lots, full refunds for unhappy buyers, and better warranties. The mom-and-pop car lots—the ones with 2 dozen dusty cars and trucks tucked between a go-kart track and an auto-parts store—will be hard-pressed to compete.

Huizenga will have imitators. CarMax, an upstart chain of used-car lots operated by Circuit City, is revving up with 5-day money-back guarantees and 30-day guarantees. Driver's Mart Worldwide plans to open 100 dealerships by 2001.

This is just one aspect of a fast-changing industry that has seen leasing, no-dicker sticker prices, and online shopping come to the fore in the 1990s.

Here's what you should do when buying a car:

1. Determine what kind of buyer you are. Let's face it: very few of us have enough cash lying around to purchase a car, which pushes us into the lease-and-used-car market. These days, Detroit subsidizes lease arrangements so dealers can offer monthly payments lower than a bank loan.

As much as leasing has going for it, I'm a skeptic. Leasing may eliminate a hefty down payment, but you will pay more in the end because you are financing more. There is no free lunch. You will also be locked into a lease that will not let you sell the car to get out in case your income falls. The best option remains paying cash.

But leasing works for the auto industry, so be prepared. The factory makes money on building the cars and then leasing them; the dealer gets his cut for being the middleman and then servicing and repairing the cars; and the dealer gets a huge supply of late-model used cars when the leased cars come back with 30,000 miles—cherry models that can be resold or released again! The dealer inspects and reconditions each used car according to a factory checklist, replacing tires, belts, brakes, and torn upholstery. These refurbished cars are then "certified" for resale and backed by extended warranties from the factory.

These developments explain why dealers are now selling more used cars than new ones—a first-ever for the industry. Another reason is price: A new car averages $20,474 versus $11,067 for a used model.

Where do you fit in? It depends on how much cash you can bring to the table. You're going to be better off paying $10,000 cash for a vehicle than putting down $10K and financing the rest, since finance charges will add several thousand dollars to the cost of the vehicle. The same idea works down the line. You're better off buying a $5,000 used car for cash rather than putting down $5K and financing $5,000.

If you can buy new, great, but you had better plan on driving it for at least seven years and 100,000 miles to get your money's worth from depreciation. If not, kick the tires of the two-year-old leased cars on the dealer lot, or look at the four-year-old cars with 60,000 miles.

Of course, you don't have to buy from a dealer, whose prices are highest. A private party is obviously cheaper, but you'll need a trusted mechanic to check the car and advise you. The other thing to do is go to the library and look up used-car prices in the *Kelley Blue Book* (it actually has a yellow cover).

2. If you do decide to buy new, remember that a new car purchase is a difficult, emotionally charged event that pits you—the inexperienced buyer—against a commissioned salesperson who does this for a living.

You can strip the emotion from the experience by not setting foot on a dealership lot until you're a "today" buyer. (You'll get asked that question at the negotiating table: "Are you a 'today' buyer?")

What car suits your family best—sedan, minivan, sports-utility vehicle, or truck? Generally speaking, models come in two versions—a regular (GS or GL) and a luxury (LX or LS). You should get a GS version with a packaged set of options—air conditioning, power locks, power windows, and so forth. You don't need the leather seats or the computerized digital displays found in the luxury models.

Next, go to the library (or online) and do your research. What do the consumer and car magazines (*Consumer Reports, Consumer Digest, Car & Driver,* and *Road & Track*) say about your dream vehicle? Also, ask friends who have that same car about their experiences.

Once you're set to shop, call the Consumer Reports New Car Pricing Service (800–933–5555) and tell them the make, model, and trim package of the vehicle you want to buy. For $12 you will receive:

- the "invoice" cost, or what the dealer paid for the car (more on that, later);
- the "sticker" price, or what the dealer wants you to pay;
- the invoice and sticker prices for all options and packages;

- current rebates, factory-to-dealer incentives, and hold-backs;
- solid advice on how to use this information to your best advantage when negotiating the purchase of your new car.

Let's say you want to buy a Mercury Villager GS minivan with the 692A package (air, power windows, and so forth). Look at the column for the base price, add the delivery charge, 692A package, and *voilá*, you have your dealer invoice price.

Keep in mind that the dealer invoice is not what the dealer *really* paid for the vehicle. That's the amount he will be *billed* by Ford, but the dealership receives a year-end "holdback" from the auto manufacturer amounting to around 3 percent of the car's invoice price.

In other words, if the dealer invoice is $25,000, he will receive a $750 bonus (if you want to call it that) from Detroit.

After educating yourself, take your test drives and walk the showroom floors. Once you sit down with the salesman, the gauntlet is down. He's listening for little verbal cues, like the time your spouse remarked, "This van will be perfect for our summer vacation" or "We have to get this in white because Dad always bought white cars."

The salesman often starts the negotiating by saying, "If I could get you this Mercury Villager for $22,500, will you buy it today?"

By saying yes, you emotionally commit to purchasing the vehicle, so don't answer affirmatively! If you do, he'll go "talk with the manager," and you know the answer will be that the dealership cannot sell you that car at that price.

Then the salesman will try to turn you into a monthly payment buyer. "How much can you afford?" he'll ask, and when you answer, you're pegging yourself, which allows the salesman to sell you the car at the price he wants.

If you resist, he'll then ask you to make a bid. At this point, you should bring out your *Consumer Reports New Car Pricing*

Guide and point out the dealer invoice price. Explain that you are willing to pay $300 above the invoice because that is what you know these cars sell for.

Be prepared to hear that Consumer Reports has the invoice numbers wrong, or that Ford recently raised its prices. Stick to your guns and remember that you don't *have* to buy the Villager from this dealership. Your greatest power is the ability to walk away.

Robert, my dealer friend, told me that good shoppers can strike deals between $200 and $500 over invoice, especially on popular four-doors such as the Taurus. "Hot" sport-utility vehicles—Ford Explorers, GM Suburbans, and Jeep Cherokees—are in shorter supply, so they command a higher premium. Either way, remember this point:

If you're paying more than $500 over invoice, the dealer is the winner. If you're paying under $500 over invoice, you're doing as well as can be expected. If you're at a "no-dicker" dealership, compare their price against your invoice.

The variable is your trade-in, and 70 percent of all sales involve one. You can work the best deal in the world and get rooked on your old car, so you need to know what it's worth. Fortunately, *Consumer Reports* can give you a verbal quote. Call 800–933–5555 again. The cost is $10.

Final point: When you're shopping for a used car, dealers have the upper hand because you can't find out what they paid for it (crazy business, isn't it?). Little wonder that dealers make more money on their used cars than on their shiny showroom models.

LESSON OF THE DAY

Don't get caught up in the new-car smell—or even the new-used-car smell. Be a cold, calculating buyer, do your complete homework before purchasing a car, and your time will be well rewarded.

The Insurance Blues

Is it payback time when it comes to auto insurance?

The phone call came shortly after New Year's day.

"I was wondering if I could drop by your house and give you a check," said Chris, my home and auto insurance agent. "I'll also be wanting to take your photo."

"My photo? Why do you want to do that?"

"Since you've gone three years without making a claim on your home or auto insurance, you've qualified to receive a rebate of $481, or 25 percent of your premiums for the past year," said Chris.

The next day, Chris asked Nicole to take a Polaroid of him handing me the check as though I were some big lotto winner.

When I told Ron Alford (author of *Auto Insurance Tricks & Repair Rip-Offs*) my little story, he scoffed.

"Here's my question," said Ron. "When you purchased your insurance, did you shop on the telephone or get written quotes?"

"Ah, I did it by telephone."

"You lose. It's impossible to buy a suit on the telephone, just as it's impossible to buy car insurance over the phone."

"What should I have done?"

"You should have gone to my Web site (*www.theplan.com*) and noodled around a bit. When you get in there, you're going to find out how to outsmart insurance agents at their own game. You're also going to find a form called an RFP—a Request for Proposal. What you do is take that form and write out exactly the kind of insurance you want for your car. Then you fax this document to a dozen different agents. Expect eight of them not to respond to you, but be happy they don't. If you do have a wreck, those are the last people you'll want to service you."

Then Ron had another question for me.

"Do you have a recovery plan in case of an accident?"

"What's that?" I asked.

"Let me set the scene," said Ron, who has this tough-guy New York accent. "You just wrecked your car. You were on your way somewhere when some idiot broadsided you. You're fine. What's the first thing that happens to you? Come on, you have no time to think. . . ."

"Call the police," I ventured.

"Good. Now what?"

"Get the other guy's driver's license number."

"Good. But do you have all your insurance information in your glove compartment?"

"I think so."

"Do you have a disposable camera in your glove box?"

"No."

"Why not?"

"I never thought about it," I confessed.

"A disposable camera is one of the most vital things you can carry. You need to take photos of your damaged car, the other guy's car, and the accident scene. Here's why. There are 65,000 collision repair companies open for business. There are about 55,000 towing companies. Most car repair and towing companies have the same address. Do you know why?"

"They want to bring business in," I guessed.

"Right," said Ron. "I have a saying for that: *Unless they have someone on the hook, there's nobody to crook.* Let's say you were not in a real bad wreck. Your car gets towed to the garage, where it gets left overnight. The next day, you have another $3,000 in damage on the car, thanks to the 'Golden Hammer.'"

"The Golden Hammer?"

"Yeah. What happens is, a collision repair worker will take a sledgehammer to your car before the insurance adjuster arrives. They want to increase their revenue stream."

When I got off the phone with Ron I felt sobered. I had not properly shopped for car insurance by asking for written quotes. I didn't have a disposable camera in my car. And I couldn't be sure if I was getting the best possible deal with American National.

I like the premise, however. American National is paying customers *not* to make a claim, although I had to go three years claim-free to get that check.

But God's timing is so interesting. One week after I talked with Ron, we got into our first accident in nearly ten years. Nicole was driving the kids down Interstate 25 when a deer jumped in front of our Villager. The glancing blow crinkled our front hood, causing $1,200 in damage, but our car was still drivable.

We didn't have a disposable camera on board, but you can be sure that I took pictures of our damaged minivan back home. We escaped the "Golden Hammer" when the car was repaired.

So, if you're going to shop for auto insurance, you can do better than I can by following these tips:

- **Ask for written quotes.** As mentioned before, you can find a Request for Proposal form at Ron's Web site or in his book *Auto Insurance Tricks & Repair Rip-offs* (call 800–THE PLAN [843–7526] to request a copy), which contains nine different profiles. You can simply copy the forms that fit you best and fax them to as many agents as possible.

Start shopping at least eight weeks before your insurance expires. Procrastinate, and you may not get the best possible rates. Decide in advance how much insurance you need and your deductible amount. A good baseline is the standard $100,000 per person—$300,000 per occurrence. You're probably going to be best off with a $500 deductible, but ask for quotes with $250 and $1,000. The numbers will tell you where to go.

You can find insurance companies by looking in the Yellow Pages. Call the office and ask for their fax number. The same goes for national companies like Geico, Allstate, and State Farm. As best as I could determine, American National Insurance (800–333–2860) is the only company offering rebates on a national level, but I'm willing to be proven wrong. For "cash back" to work, however, the rates have to be competitive. It doesn't make sense to overpay on car insurance just to get a rebate, and besides, it's a gamble that you'll be able to go three years claim-free.

- **Realize that you can receive different quotes even within the same company.** Call fifteen different Farmer's agents, the joke goes, and you'll receive fifteen different quotes.
- **Check the policy after you receive it.** If you get quoted $1,050 to insure two cars, it may take six to eight weeks before the policy lands in your mailbox—enough time for you to have forgotten the quote. That's why you need it in writing. Ron Alford has heard of too many cases in which another 10 percent gets added on.

You also need to check your policy for errors. In my last statement, I noticed that I had been charged for collision insurance on my fifteen-year-old GMC pickup that's only worth a couple thousand dollars. I wonder how many times I paid without doublechecking my policy?

- **Determine whether it's a good deal to "gang up" your home and auto insurance.** Ron Alford says you don't save. "What insurance companies are doing is getting all your money instead of some of it," he said. But some companies claim the discount to bring your auto and home under the same umbrella can total 5–10 percent. See it in writing first.
- **Be honest with the insurance agent.** You should know that insurance companies belong to CLUE—the Comprehensive Loss Underwriting Exchange. They share information on accident claims, so if you fib and get turned down by the new insurance firm, your *old* company will hear about that.
- **Drop collision insurance if your car is worth less than $3,000.** If you get in a wreck, you'll have to pay for all the repairs or have the car towed to the salvage yard. But the Lord can protect us!
- **Ask for the low mileage discount.** If you drive one of your cars 7,500 miles or less annually, you can receive a lower quote. Again, be honest.
- **It may pay to stay with a company as long as you can.** Some insurance firms offer a "preferred" discount— around 10–15 percent—for customers who go three, five, or six years accident-free.
- **Have your credit cards paid up.** More and more insurance companies are running credit checks, which they use to determine how much to charge. Allstate says individuals with bad credit are 250 percent more likely to have an accident, a vehicle stolen, or file a fraudulent claim. Guess what? Those with bad credit get quoted higher rates.
- **If you're a military family, go with USAA.** From what I hear, USAA is tough to beat, but you have to have served in the military or be a military dependent.
- **Do everything you can to avoid a claim.** That means paying for repairs under your deductible and even for repairs

several hundred dollars *above* your deductible. In Colorado, windshields constantly crack from rocks and gravel. If you have a windshield to replace, standard sedans cost around $125 to $250, while minivans with large, sloped windshields can be over $500. Once windshield companies learn you are a "cash customer," however, it's amazing how fast they can drop their price.

- **Watch your driving habits.** Most accidents are caused by driving too close to the car in front of you. Back off. The other danger point is left-hand turns. Let's say you're poised to make a left-hand turn against three lanes of traffic. It's rush hour, so cars are backed up. If a driver on the other side of the road is stopped, sees you wanting to make a left, and waves his hand for you to proceed, don't go! You often can't see traffic barreling down the other two lanes.

  The other situation involves making a left turn as the light turns yellow. Watch for cars running the red light! In most states, you will be the one at fault.

- **If you have teenage drivers, share your car with them instead of buying another car, because it will cost a bundle to insure that vehicle.** Sure, it's a hassle to share, but you're saving $150–$300 a month.

- **Don't skimp on driver's education.** Although private driving schools cost between $250 and $600, your child's safety—and your peace of mind—is worth the cost. You can often qualify for an insurance discount when your teen passes driver's ed, and you'll also receive a lower quote if your teen goes off to college.

LESSON OF THE DAY

You'll be in good hands when you shop auto and home insurance well.

You Bet Your Life

Purchase life insurance that goes the term

The middle-aged insurance agent watched earnestly while I paged through a prospectus that plotted my insurance needs.

"This will provide for your family in case you're no longer here," he informed me.

You mean when I'm dead, I thought.

My head swam from all the figures and projections and expected payouts, but there was one figure I understood: This "whole" life insurance policy would cost me close to $3,600 a year, or $300 a month.

That sealed my decision, since I didn't have anywhere near an extra three hundred bucks a month to work with. Then I remembered something: my retirement plan with Focus on the Family was better than any life insurance product because the ministry matched employee contributions up to 5 percent of our salaries. (We are expected to self-manage our retirement accounts, however.)

The light went on. For the first time, I actually understood what whole life, variable life, and any other "piece of the rock" insurance was all about: my premiums were really an investment account with the insurance company, for which I received a death benefit and a return on my investment. When I studied the numbers in the folder, I realized that I was being guaranteed 4.5 percent on my money—as long as I paid in for seven years. (I've later learned that the insurance agent's commission eats up most of your premiums in the first seven years.)

"I don't think your insurance policy with savings can beat my retirement program here at Focus," I told the agent. "I receive a 100 percent return the first year because Focus matches my contribution. I don't think your company can offer me a 100 percent return on my money."

The agent mulled that one for a moment. When he saw there wasn't anything more to discuss, he picked up his leather satchel and was gone.

In a sense, there really isn't anything to discuss regarding life insurance, because you'll do just fine by doing two things:

1. Buy low-cost term life insurance on yourself (if you are the family's breadwinner).
2. Invest in your company's retirement program or contribute to an IRA.

Simply put, term life insurance is a voluntary arrangement between you and the insurance company, based on whether you'll be alive at year's end. If you're not around, a death benefit is paid, and your policy became the most cost-efficient way to provide for your family when the Lord took you home.

If you are a 30-year-old nonsmoking male, you can purchase a $250,000 policy for $173 a year in a 10-year-level policy. (That means your benefit stays the same over 10 years. The policy costs a little more in the first year or two, but when paid out over a decade represents a significant savings.)

The term life insurance field is competitive and easy to shop, thanks to 800-numbers. One of the joys of purchasing term life is that it can all be done over the phone; no salesman ever steps inside your house.

How much life insurance should you have?

"It is my experience and judgment that eight times Dad's annual income is the moral minimum purchase," said David Holmes, my life insurance agent. "Your family should be able to maintain its current lifestyle with a 12 percent return on that lump sum."

I saw David's advertisement in *World* magazine, a Christian publication, and after David shopped the best rate among AA-rated companies, he set me up with a ten-year-level plan.

"In 1 Timothy 5:8," said David, "God cautions us to make provisions: 'If anyone does not provide for his relatives, and especially for his immediate family, he has denied the faith and is worse than an unbeliever' (NIV). Godly men prepare spiritual and physical inheritances for their wives, children, and grandchildren. There is not a working dad in America who cannot afford all the life insurance his family will need."

Indeed, 10-, 15-, and 20-year level term life insurance rates have remained steady in the last couple of years, so there is *no* excuse for not being covered. To get the best rates:

- **You need to be in great health.** That means not using any tobacco products in the last three years, no risky employment, no risky foreign business travel, and a good health record. Insurance companies require a blood test to screen you for existing medical conditions (diabetes, leukemia, HIV, and so on). This is how they keep their rates down since they will not insure sick people at a low rate. Companies that do *not* require a blood test will be charging you more—that's a guarantee.
- **If you're under 40 years of age, shop for a 10-year or 20-year level plan.** You can save 20–25 percent this way. But

what would happen if you near the end of your 10-year level plan and your doctor, during a routine checkup, discovers that you have prostate cancer? This is when you will wish you had a whole-life policy. This is not the time to leave your present insurance company because you probably could not land with another. But good news: even though your 10-year-level plan has ended, the insurance company cannot cancel you! The insurance company will, however, jack up your annual premiums since they have no idea how healthy you are. But at least you and your family will be covered as you battle the cancer.

- **Go to the phones for the best quote.** The David Holmes Agency can be reached by calling (800) 327–8963. Other companies to call for free quotes are: LifeQuotes (800–441–0072), InsuranceQuote (800–972–1104), Select Quote (800–343–1985), Veritas (800–552–3553), and Quotesmith (800–556–9393).
- **Direct-mail life insurance quotes aren't the cheapest.** (The same goes for those late-night TV ads.) One pitch in my cable TV statement offered me the standard $250,000 term-life for $825. Such a deal.
- **Drop life insurance after the age of 65.** Think about it: If you die after age 65, what happens? Well, your surviving spouse inherits the estate, which should be enough to see her through, especially if you have a retirement nest egg. Besides, term life insurance in the retirement years costs close to $2,000 a year for a 10-year level plan.

INSURANCE YOU DON'T NEED

Because insurance is profitable business, you'll get hit up to insure everything from calamities to your children. Here are some insurance products to avoid like the plague:

- **Life insurance on your wife (if she doesn't work outside the home).** Before you start tossing bricks my way, the cost to insure against your wife's death defeats the reason why you buy insurance, which is to provide a family with income in case the breadwinner dies.

- **If you do have a whole-life policy, watch out for a second hit.** If an agent calls and says he can get you more insurance for little or no extra cost, you will actually be taking a hidden loan against the cash value of your old policy— or "churning" those dollars. Unfortunately, when your cash values are used up, your policy lapses. Use "surrenderable additions," *not* the cash value, to buy more.

- **Disability insurance.** Disability insurance sounds great— who wouldn't want to be insured in case one loses an eye or becomes disabled following a car accident? But in my opinion, the rates are too high to replace 60–65 percent of your income. If you earn $30,000 a year, you'll have to pay 2 percent to be covered, or $50 a month. That's a lot for a policy written with loopholes.

- **Mortgage life insurance.** This pays off your mortgage in the event of your death, which is just another way of buying term life insurance for the amount of your mortgage. Capstead, my mortgage company, offered me $123,000 coverage for $339 a year, whereas I can get *double* that amount of life insurance—$250,000—for $236 a year. Adding my wife would be another $204 a year. Yikes!

- **Credit card insurance.** This product pays off your credit card balances in the event of your untimely demise. Like mortgage insurance, these premiums are 50–75 percent higher than term life. They are mainly marketed to those who can't qualify for regular life insurance, since they don't have you take a blood test.

- **Accidental death, double indemnity, or "dread disease" insurance.** These policies are no better than shooting craps with the insurance company. What are the chances of dying in a car wreck, plane crash, or smacking into a tree while skiing? Very, very low. Double indemnity means that the insurance company will pay double the face value if you die accidentally. Do you want to pay $150 a year for this policy? Dread-disease policies will help pay medical expenses for certain diseases such as cancer, but adequate medical insurance should have you covered.

• **Skip the flight insurance.** I can remember as a young boy in the early sixties watching my mom drop one of those "Mutual of Omaha" life insurance plans in the airport mailbox just before we boarded every flight. Then a couple of years ago, Mom bought another Mutual of Omaha policy before a memorable trip to Hawaii. Feelings of nostalgia aside, the $150,000 policy was overpriced, even at $5.

LESSON OF THE DAY

Insurance salespeople play on your emotions, giving you a huge guilt trip. Step back, keep a cool head, and purchase the right amount of term life insurance for your family.

When You Gotta See a Doctor

Know who's paying before you leave the house

A couple of years ago, Nicole developed a crick in her neck that wouldn't go away. Our family doctor referred her to a physical therapist, who kneaded Nicole's neck muscles and upper spine twice weekly for a couple of months.

Nicole's treatments were covered by our medical insurance, but we were still billed for out-of-pocket expenses such as co-pays and what was *not* covered by insurance. Our portion came to $200.

We never figured out why Nicole's neck hurt until one afternoon while she was ironing. The telephone rang, so Nicole—trying to be as efficient with her time as possible—cradled the cordless phone between her shoulder and left ear while she continued to press my dress shirts.

That's when she discovered why her neck hurt so much.

Another pain in the neck is medical insurance. The cost of medical care is beyond comprehension, and there is very little we can do about it.

The explanation lies in the way that health care has evolved in the last fifty years. Two generations ago, when families were paying their own doctor bills, the family-to-doctor relationship acted as a "governor" to keep prices down. But as third-party insurance companies entered the scene, there was not much financial incentive for doctors and hospitals to keep costs reasonable. The next evolution occurred when fantastic medical advances reached the public in the form of ultrasound, MRI, and CAT-scan machines, and surgeries such as organ transplants and quadruple bypasses became routine. Under those circumstances, who would want to return to the old days?

There's another issue at play. When a child is very sick or recovering from a terrible accident, no parent would "shop" doctors for the best price. In fact, we would empty our bank accounts to get the best medical care possible.

Still, something has to be done about spiraling costs, which is why we saw Hillary Clinton advance her government-funded health care plan in 1993. Since her defeat, market forces are being brought to bear, and we are seeing the growth of "managed care," which means insurance companies are working hard to drive down costs.

In addition, we're starting to see more and more businesses that are "self-insured" and pay medical claims for their employees. That means it's *your* company paying for that gallbladder surgery, not some third-party insurance company back in Hartford, Connecticut.

If your company doesn't offer medical insurance or you are self-employed, you will need to purchase insurance with high deductibles of $2,000 or $5,000. You will have to pay for all office visits and the kids' stitches, but these high-deductible policies can lower an astronomical $800-a-month premium to something more reasonable, such as $200 or less for a family of four.

KNOW WHAT YOUR INSURANCE PAYS FOR!

One thing I can't stress enough is the paramount importance of reading your Group Benefits plan. If you don't seek pre-authorization for outpatient surgeries or stay within your "preferred-provider" network of doctors, you will be liable for what is not covered under your employee plan.

I nearly had a heart attack following surgery on my left foot. The procedure took three hours in an outpatient surgical center, which I thought was "inside" the PPO system. Then I received a dunning $900 bill from the surgical center for services rendered. I quickly called my doctor's office, who assured me that the surgical center was wrong. I didn't breathe easily until my bill was dropped.

Insurance companies are trying to steer parents away from taking their children to the emergency room for a sore throat. According to my Group Benefits book, I will pay $75 for each emergency room visit, while an off-hours visit to a satellite "emergicare" facility is just a $15 co-pay. You know where I will be going if my son, Patrick, gouges his knee.

"Going to the emergency room is very costly," said Cathy Blackwood, whose husband, Robb, is a family practitioner and member of the Focus on the Family Physicians Resource Council. "Always make it a point to see your family doctor rather than making that trip to the ER." Cathy is a mother of ten children who has dealt with her share of sick children and stitches over the years.

Cathy says families should develop a close relationship with their family doctor, who has become the point person under this new "managed care" system.

How does it work? Let's say you have a history of migraine headaches, but suddenly your 12-year-old daughter develops a bad headache. If you were to take your crying child to the emergency room, the on-duty ER doc could very well order up a CAT scan or MRI—procedures that cost over $1,000. On the other hand, your family doctor would know about the history of migraines in your family, and he or she would make treatment plans accordingly.

I've always relied on word-of-mouth for finding a good family doctor, but Cathy says be sure to check if your family doctor is board-certified or board-eligible, which means he or she is keeping up with the medical profession through continuing education.

"Having a good relationship means you can call your doctor on minor things and save an office visit," said Cathy.

"Really?" I asked. "Isn't that being cheap?"

"Not at all," replied Cathy. "Robb has patients call him all the time, and he recognizes that this is one way he can help people."

Dr. Tom Fitch, a pediatrician from San Antonio, Texas, and also a member of Focus on the Family's Physicians Resource Council, told me that he doesn't mind when patients call him. "We don't make money on patient calls, but that's okay," he said. "If we can handle it on the phone, fine. There's no sense in having someone come in who doesn't need to."

I would counsel you not to overdo it when calling your doctor. Use the Golden Rule: *Would you mind being called if you were the doctor?*

Another area that people try to save money in is free drug samples. "You can ask for them, but doctors often reserve those free drugs for destitute families," said Dr. Robb Blackwood. "One thing you should ask for is generic drugs on your prescriptions."

Over-the-counter generic versions of Advil, Tylenol, and aspirin can also save money. "If you look at the dosage of the drug in the generic product," said Robb, "you will notice that it's exactly the same as the name brand. It's just not packaged as nicely. But I would avoid a lot of the over-the-counter cold medicines, the orange and purple kinds, because they don't do much for your money."

Cathy reminds parents that the common cold and flu bugs often run their course after twenty-four or thirty-six hours, so don't be in a hurry to take your children in for an office visit. Wait several days, and if symptoms persist, then it's time.

As for flu shots, I think they're great. I've taken them for several years, and I've missed only a couple of days of work during the flu season.

GOOD PREVENTIVE MEDICINE

Dr. Fitch believes in preventive care. For your children, this means giving them their polio, DPT, measles, mumps, and rubella shots. "People who don't have insurance can go to the public health department and get their immunizations," said Dr. Fitch. "The charge is minimal because our tax dollars are paying for them. Those who can afford it or have insurance should not use taxpayer dollars to get their immunizations, however."

For *your* good health, preventive care means regular check-ups and flu shots. "I've seen mothers and fathers skimp on their own check-ups, but those check-ups give us a chance to pick up things early. We just might be able to help you prevent a heart attack or stroke," said Dr. Fitch.

"You will also get more for your dollar if you do not have three other children running around the exam room, interfering with the doctor. If possible, get someone to watch your children. You should also come prepared with questions you want to ask."

But there's one more preventive medical issue we should talk about. If we can inculcate our children with God's Word and biblical values, we can help them avoid sinful behavior that will put their health at risk.

"Preventive medicine is talking to our kids about sex," said Dr. Fitch. "I would encourage parents to use Dr. Dobson's book, *Preparing for Adolescence* just before their kids become teenagers. That book can have a tremendous payback down the line in helping your child say no to drugs, premarital sex, and peer pressure."

And that will be just what the doctor ordered.

LESSON OF THE DAY

Your family library won't be complete until you bring home the recently released Complete Child and Baby Care Book *(Tyndale), which was written by Focus on the Family's Physicians Resource Council. This 986-page volume is the Christian response to Dr. Spock, and it is filled with hundreds of preventive medical tips.*

Virtual Shopping

Is shopping on the Internet the wave of the future?

It was Saturday night, and all the stores were closed. Kale Burnham, an eighth-grader, suddenly remembered that Mother's Day was just hours away.

What should he do? Kale couldn't drive, and he certainly couldn't ask his mother, Pam, to chauffeur him to the local supermarket to at least buy some flowers. Then Kale had an idea.

The 14-year-old boy settled before the family computer and dialed into the Internet. Kale, who made up his own Web page one night, easily moved his cursor to "Bookmarks," where he clicked on *www.geocities.com/GreetingCards*. Within minutes, he customized a Mother's Day card and ordered a bouquet of virtual flowers to be dropped into his mom's e-mail box.

When Pam checked her e-mail the next morning and noticed the virtual flowers and card in her inbox, she nearly burst into tears.

"It was so touching," she told me. "And it was certainly the right price for Kale."

Yes, the flowers and card were free because they existed only in cyberspace. But you can send *real* flowers and a card by dialing *www.800flowers.com.* "I sent my mom flowers for Mother's Day that way," said Pam. "I'm just too busy to battle the crowds."

Pam is a working mom who's been in the computer industry since 1970, when she started as a programmer. Those were the days when a huge room of IBM computers had the same firepower as an off-the-shelf laptop computer these days. She headed Focus on the Family's Management Information Services department before leaving the ministry to become a consultant to American Express.

Pam has been shopping in the Internet since the early 1990s—long before I ever heard of the World Wide Web. Whether we're ready to embrace this technology or not, it's being invented right before our eyes. Web merchandising sales were $500 million in 1996, but analysts are confident that that total will leap to $5 billion or more by the year 2000. "Just as the automobile, telephone, and airplane shortened the cycles of human commerce and relationships in the first half of the century," wrote Eric Garland in *Adweek* magazine, "the Web is collapsing the most basic state of economic relations—buying and selling—as the next century starts."

Garland is right. Goods and services like books, CDs, computer hardware and software, and travel information are taking the Web by storm. Stuff that people need to see and touch—cars, clothes, jewelry—will be a more difficult sale.

Pam Burnham showed me her favorite Web shopping site, Amazon Books (*www.amazon.com*). Amazon Books exists in cyberspace, and while it advertises one million titles, it only stocks best-sellers and other books in demand. If you request a book not in stock (another copy of *21 Days to a Thrifty Lifestyle*, perhaps?) they will special-order it, which means it may arrive in your mailbox one to three weeks later.

"But Amazon tries to make it easy for you," said Pam. "When I order something, I have an e-mail the next day notifying me that they received my order and giving me my confirmation number. When they ship it, they send me another e-mail. That's nice."

Another of Pam's favorite sites is JCPenney. The department store has a virtual "clearance rack," but you can't try anything on, of course. I don't know if Pam was serious or not, but she hopes that one day you'll be able to put a picture of yourself on the screen and have clothes "tried on" right before your eyes.

One advantage of the Internet is that you can use "chat rooms" to find the best deal *outside* the Web. When I wanted to buy more RAM memory for my home computer, I clicked America Online's computer icon and punched into a discussion group area. I joined the fracas, posing as a neophyte who knew nothing about computers but knew I needed more RAM. *Can anyone help me?*

Within minutes, my newfound cyberfriends tapped in the names and 800-numbers for several RAM memory companies. I used those numbers to shop the best deal and then purchased thirty-two megs of RAM at almost half off the going rate at CompUSA!

I'm going to make a few observations about shopping on the Internet, which has a bright future. At this time, however, you should know a few things.

1. **You won't save money.** I don't mean that you *can't* save money, but from what Pam has shown me, the cost of books, CDs, clothes, shoes, and flowers are about what you'd pay at normal retail prices. Amazon may sell their books for a couple of dollars less than full markup, but that margin is eaten up by the ubiquitous "shipping and handling" fees. Ditto for CDs, which can be had for $14.99 on the Net. I expect prices to go

down as cybershopping expands and companies learn what sells and what doesn't.

What Internet companies are selling is convenience. You don't have to get in a car and go down to a flower store to send flowers to Mom. If you're a two-income household, time is more valuable than saving a few dollars, and Web companies have tapped into that need.

2. **You can save money.** As mentioned with my RAM memory experience, you *can* use the Web to find the mail-order companies that offer fantastic prices. Those companies are out there; you just have to find them. Use search engines such as Yahoo and Metacrawler to find these companies by typing in a key word. Discussion groups can be very helpful, as I mentioned.

3. **You need a speedy modem.** One of my gripes with "surfing the Net" is that the waves break awfully slowly. I have a 33.6 kilobaud-per-second modem, and it still takes too long for the various Web pages to pop up. That downside is being addressed. Pam Burnham said when Internet commerce began, companies felt a need to put a lot of graphic elements on their Web page, but that slowed down the pages coming up. The graphics are rather bare bones today, and many Web pages have buttons to take you where you want to go, instead of clicking on page after page.

The new 56.6 kps modems are supposed to make Internet cruising faster than ever, but many Internet service providers are hemmed in by the limitations of local phone lines.

A technology in the not-so-distant future, called TVP, will give us relative lightning speed, and it may even supplant long-distance phone charges. The day is not long off when my wife, Nicole, who was born and raised in Switzerland and still has all her family there, will be able to go on the Internet, speak into the computer—and be heard by her family in the "old country"!

The cost would be included in the monthly price of unlimited Internet service, which can be had for $15 to $20 a month.

Can you imagine making all the long-distance phone calls you want—for as long as you want—for less than 20 bucks a month?

- **Watch for Internet airline tickets.** This is an area of the Internet that I think has the most potential, although it's not there yet. If you think about it, Internet tickets are a natural for the airlines. Once that unfilled seat is in the air, it's worth nothing. Why not try to get *something* for that seat at the last minute?

  American Airlines and TWA have started selling Internet tickets, and I expect many airlines to follow. When I signed up I started receiving e-mail messages each Wednesday notifying me of the specials for the upcoming weekend. Departures could take place only on Thursday, Friday, or Saturday, with a Monday or Tuesday return.

  Usually only a couple of dozen routes are put on sale—New York-Atlanta, or Dallas-San Diego, plus some international flights. Prices are excellent and cheaper than any price-war fares, but then again, we're talking about a very short trip on very short notice. I've seen prices of $129 for a roundtrip between Atlanta and Denver, or $299 from New York to Paris. But even if you left on Thursday afternoon for Paris and returned Tuesday, you'd have fewer than three jet-lagged days in the City of Light.

  The biggest thing working against these cyberfares is that they only work if you live near a major airline's hub, such as New York, Los Angeles, Dallas, Atlanta, or in the case of TWA, St. Louis.

- **Remember that companies are struggling to find profitability on the Internet.** The demand for Internet shopping is not high, but as a critical mass forms, Web shopping will be something that traditional retailers will have to contend with.

- **Finally, here are some top Internet sites.** Please note that I have dropped the http://www prefix:

  For shopping: *llbean.com*; *JCPenney.com*

  For travel: *americanexpress.com*; *travelocity.com*; *vacations.com*; *travelweb.com*; and *expedia.msn.com*

  For airlines: *americanair.com*; *ual.com*; *nwa.com*; *flycontinental.com*; *twa.com*

LESSON OF THE DAY

There are hundreds, if not thousands, of Internet sites worth checking out, and new ones are being introduced each day. Computer magazines will help you keep abreast of this fast-changing medium.

Gimme Credit

It's time we rethink how we use credit cards

I'm going to start off this chapter with a little speech:

If you have an outstanding balance on your credit cards, then you must do everything you can to get your credit cards paid off.

I don't know how this type of thinking began, but the following is the mindset of many Americans regarding credit cards, department store cards, and consumer loans: *This is not a bill. You're not expected to pay in full. Just send in the minimum payment, and everything will be okay.*

Around two-thirds of American families don't pay off their balances every month, which means they keep on truckin' down the highway of debt at double-digit annual interest. The average household has four credit cards with balances totalling $4,800, up from two cards and $2,340 in balances just five years ago. If you're one of those families, you're traveling in the wrong direction.

To turn things around, you're going to have to work overtime or take a second job, or send your spouse back to the workforce. (If you're both working and in some serious debt, I would recommend financial counseling.) Remember: You can't be saving for retirement or throwing a few extra dollars at your mortgage when 18 percent credit-card interest is financially eating you alive.

If I've pricked your conscience to finally do *something*, take a small Tupperware bowl, fill it with water, and drop your credit cards in. Then place the Tupperware in your freezer. That way you can't use them unless it's *really* an emergency.

Paying cash or using your checkbook will be difficult, but you'll get used to it. Then you can get working on those credit cards. Mary Hunt of *Cheapskate Monthly* has a great "Rapid Debt-Repayment Plan" to pay off installment debt. Here's what you do:

1. Add up all your current required monthly minimum payments on your credit cards, store charge cards, installment loans (for furniture, TVs, and so forth) and any personal loans (like college loans). Let's say those minimum amounts add up to $300. Commit to paying that amount each month toward your debts until they are all paid off. If the total is too steep, then contact each credit card company and ask for a temporary payment reduction.

2. List your debts in order of the number of months left to pay them off. Put the one with the shortest term to pay off at the top of the list. While still making payments on your other debts, throw your extra money against that debt on the top of your list.

3. When the shortest debt is paid off, add its payment to the next shortest. Do the same until that $300 amount you committed to pay each month is applied to your last debt.

This is just a short outline of Mary's "Rapid Debt-Repayment Plan." You can call her office at (562) 630–8845 for a chart that will walk you through the process.

WHEN YOU ARE PAID UP

I don't think it's any coincidence that credit-card debt per household doubled in the 1990s, just as banks and credit-card companies began issuing a slew of "rebate" cards that earn you frequent flier miles, discounts on Ford and GM cars, GE appliances, Toys-R-Us products, Shell gas, Quaker State oil, T.J. Maxx apparel, Blockbuster movies—even cash back. If you're among the other one-third of households who *do* pay off those nasty credit-card bills each month, there are some good pickings out there.

Do these come-ons work? Sure, but you have to study *which* card will work best for your family. For most families it's a "co-branding" card that links purchases to frequent flyer miles with a major airline: Spend a buck, get a mile. We signed up for an American Airlines AAdvantage Citibank Visa card in the spring of 1992, and after 3 years we had racked up enough miles to earn two round-trip tickets to Switzerland for Christmas of 1995. The cost of those plane tickets from Denver to Zurich would have been around $1,000 each, so I received a $2,000 benefit minus 3 years of annual fees ($150). I'd say that was a good deal.

But it's a game. I signed up for a free American West credit card just to receive the 5,000 bonus miles. I never used the card. I even requested a Blockbuster card since they promised a half-dozen free video rentals. That card has been canceled.

Before jumping in, you have to ask yourself: *Do I spend enough each month to justify one of these rebate cards?* You probably will, although you will have to be rather intentional about putting *all* your purchases on the card, since the goal is to earn a round-trip airline ticket (or free oil changes or whatever).

If you make purchases that are reimbursed, so much the better, since it's like earning "free" miles. Mark Thurlow, who works for the Navigators in Colorado Springs, does a lot of company mailings, which he pays for with his personal credit card and is then reimbursed. He earns 2,000 free miles a month. If I'm out at a restaurant with friends and the bill comes to the table, I have no trouble putting the entire amount on my card and collecting cash from my friends.

If you want to jump in, remember these caveats:

- **You will spend more by using a credit card than by paying cash.** Christian financial counselor Ron Blue says families spend 34 percent more with a credit card versus cash, and I believe him. Nicole and I have always had the mindset that what we're charging today *must* be paid for next month, but some of our monthly Visa statements have us saying, "When did we charge that?"

  You see, if your goal is to accumulate "points" or miles, it's easy to charge nearly everything these days. Supermarkets, gas stations—even ministries like Focus on the Family—accept credit cards. The major phone companies, such as AT&T, MCI, and Sprint, reward you with five miles for every dollar in phone charges.

- **Use only one credit card.** Even though I've requested second cards over the years, I've never used them. It's rather complicated to track the spending on one card, let alone two or three. I put my credit-card purchases in my Quicken program, so when we hit our personal limit, we can slam the brakes on our spending. Since our billing month closes on the 24th of each month, Nicole and I have delayed some purchases so they wouldn't show up until the next month's statement.

- **Don't get department store cards.** You don't need them. Every department store in the world accepts Visa or

Mastercard, so what's the benefit in using a Nordstrom's card?

- **Be willing to switch credit card companies.** For the last couple of years, the credit-card issuers have been reducing incentives and reining in benefits. This is partly because more families are stiffing them and declaring bankruptcy, and partly because they want to preserve profits. The GE Rewards card started slapping a $25 annual fee on holders who had the audacity to pay their bill in full every month! Nearly all the airlines raised the domestic flight award from 20,000 to 25,000 miles in 1995, and Ford stopped its rebate program that cardholders used toward buying or leasing a new Fort car or truck.

That's why I recently switched from Citibank Visa's American Airlines card to AAA Member Select Rewards card (888–AAA–5502). Yes, you do have to be a AAA member, but you receive a round-trip domestic ticket within the 48 states on United or Continental Airlines for 16,000 points (you get a point for every dollar you charge). Nearly all the other airlines require 25,000 miles.

The AAA card requires 36 percent fewer miles to gain a free flight. As with most "rewards" cards, the AAA card has an annual fee of $50.

If the AAA Member Select Rewards Card doesn't work for you (perhaps you're not close to an airport with United and Continental flights), then I recommend one of the airline cards. The major players are American Airlines AAdvantage (800–843–0777), United Mileage Plus (800–537–7783), Continental One Pass (800–446–5336), and Northwest (800–945–2004).

If the airline cards don't fly with you, know that I do *not* recommend American Express and Diners Club since they are not widely accepted, especially in supermarkets and regular stores. The Discover Card offers cash back, but not very much. Spending

$16,000, for example, earns you a rebate of only $145, far less than the cost of a transcontinental ticket.

LESSON OF THE DAY

Be very careful when using a credit card.
Reserve the cash in your checking account
and pay the balance in full every month.
Otherwise you lose!

DAY 16

I'll Fly Away

Fly the friendly skies for fewer dollars

I am not a professional traveler, and I do not pretend to know the ins and outs of a turbulent industry that sends 20,000 flights into the air each day.

Our vacation dollars pay for flights to see the family—and little else, which is fine with me, because my parents and Nicole's parents mean so much so us. Today I'm not going to tell you how to shop for puka shells in Honolulu or where budget hotels can be found in Paris. Instead, I will share some strategies for saving big bucks on air travel:

1. Plan ahead. No, make that: plan *way* ahead. If you're going to see family—especially during a holiday time—you'd better firm up plans six months out. I've purchased Christmas tickets in July and reserved frequent flier tickets to Switzerland *eleven* months in advance. Good communication between you and your family will allow you to go after discount fares when the airlines suddenly fire another salvo in their periodic price wars.

2. Anticipate fare wars. Fare wars strike several times during the year. March and April are the months when summer sales are held. What the airlines are saying is this: *If you'll tie up your money with us for three to six months, we'll let you book your summer holiday.*

Deep discounts are advertised after Labor Day for travel up until Christmas, and just after the New Year you can find winter and spring fares good until Memorial Day weekend. Don't expect dynamite deals to Orlando in the month of February, however.

You find out about airfare wars by looking for advertisements in major newspapers or *USA Today*, or by staying in steady phone contact with your travel agent.

3. Become best buddies with your travel agent. Since the airlines post over 100,000 rate changes each day (incredible!), you can't expect an agent to call you if the price of a flight from Pittsburgh to San Francisco suddenly drops from $448 to $249.

When airlines slash prices they are practicing "seat management," in which computers set the prices based on anticipated demand. If sales are slow for a particular flight, the computer stimulates sales by tweaking the rates. I've had travel agents— the good ones—tell me they don't mind if I call in each day. They know the game.

4. Be your own travel agent. I am not contradicting myself. If you are computer savvy, you can browse the SABRE system on the Internet, or you can deal directly with the airlines when you hear about an airfare war. Just a handful of seats are held out for the sale price, so it may be better to call right away rather than to wait until morning and having your agent book.

If you're trying to build frequent flier miles on a certain airline, call them to see if they are matching the competitor's sale.

The airlines often do—right down to the dollar and the booking restrictions.

5. Find out when "off-peak" times are. Flights that are convenient for business travelers—who pay the freight for the airlines—are early in the morning and late afternoon. Naturally, the computers are going to keep the fares on those flights higher. But traveling before 7:00 A.M., late morning, early afternoon, or after 8:00 P.M., can result in significant savings.

Then there are "peak" and "off-peak" *days*. Don't expect to get the deal of the century on Thanksgiving Eve. You might be able to fly cheap at 7:00 A.M. on Wednesday morning, however. Is it worth it to take the kids out of school? Certainly! Not much gets done that day anyway.

Ditto for a return flight on the Sunday after Thanksgiving, or flights at the beginning and end of Christmas vacation. If you fly a little off-kilter, you can get a good price—provided you purchase months ahead.

6. Read the tiny ads in the Sunday travel section. Those two-inch square ads found in the travel sections of big-city newspapers are usually from consolidators, or wholesale travel companies that buy blocks of seats from regularly scheduled airlines and then resell them on the open market. If they don't sell the tickets, they're stuck.

Mary VanMeer, publisher of the *Thrifty Traveler Newsletter* (800–532–5731), always travels on consolidators' tickets from her home near Tampa, Florida, but advises travelers to stick with reputable consolidators. The best one, she says, is TFI Tours International (800–745–8000); they sell domestic fares, too.

When I called TFI to check them out, I asked in June for seats from Denver to Zurich in either July, August, or September. The soonest TFI could find available seats was September for a price of $670 roundtrip. That's not bad for off-season, but TFI did not have the tickets I wanted during the height of summer. I would have had to call earlier in the spring.

Some of the reputable, well-established consolidators are:

Domestic

- Cheap Seats (800–451–7200)
- 1-800-FLY-ASAP (800–359–2727)
- 1-800-FLY-CHEAP (800–359–2432)

International

- Travac (800–800–TRAV)
- Travel Bargains (800–872–8385)
- UniTravel (800–325–2222)

7. On short-haul flights, support your local discount airline. Without the little guys, the Big Boys—American, Delta, United, Northwest, and USAir—would have the runways all to themselves, and you'd be much lighter in the pocketbook. A friend of mine, Tom Mason, told me that before the ValuJet crash in 1996 he could purchase $104 roundtrip tickets for a Delta flight from Atlanta to Dallas. Delta was merely matching ValuJet on that route.

Following the tragic crash, which grounded ValuJet, fares shot up to $440. "You'd think there would be a middle ground," said Tom.

Not in the airline business.

The best discount airline is one I've never had the pleasure of flying: Southwest Airlines. Southwest doesn't fly into Colorado, but I hear that Southwest consistently has the best fares from Point A to Point B, and the airline consistently has the best on-time performance and customer service. We need to keep the Southwests of the world profitable.

8. Be willing to fly red-eyes. A daunting prospect, especially with kids, but if a middle-of-the-night flight saves the family several hundred dollars, you're being paid well for an evening of sleep deprivation. Maybe you'll get lucky and the kids will sleep.

9. Consider driving to a different airport. When Western Pacific, a discount airline, began operations in Colorado Springs, you should have seen the number of Denver folks traveling south on I-25 to the Springs airport.

Of course, it has to be worth your time to drive out of your way to another airport. But if a two-hour journey saves the family several hundred dollars on a cross-country fare, make the drive.

10. If you need to travel in a hurry, go with the consolidators. If you have to fly quickly to be at a parent's bedside, consolidators sell tickets that do not have the standard 21-day advance purchase requirement. If you need a bereavement fare following the death of a loved one, check that fare against those of the consolidators.

11. Volunteer to get bumped. When you check in for a busy flight, tell the agent your family is willing to be "bumped" to make room for late-arriving passengers. The airline will usually put you on the next available flight and compensate you with vouchers for future travel.

12. Complain when flights go wrong. When an airline messes up—canceling a flight, sitting on the tarmac for three hours, leaving you stranded overnight in some faraway hub—write a letter. Patiently but forthrightly describe what happened and ask if there is anything the airline can do to rectify the situation.

My complaints—all legitimate—have netted me thousands of frequent flier miles and discount vouchers good for future flights. The airlines want to keep you happy: American Airlines, in a survey, learned that each unhappy passenger tells nine to thirteen people about his or her bad experience.

13. When going on vacation, stay with family and friends. Family is family, but when we've stayed with friends, we've tried to be the best guests ever—cooking meals, helping with the clean-up, taking out trash, and even mowing lawns. By staying out of motels and coffee shops, we have saved an easy $100 a day.

14. Rent a condominium. A one- or two-bedroom condo is comparably priced to a standard hotel room with two double beds, yet condos have full kitchen facilities. Cooking for yourself—or at least eating breakfast and snacking in your condo—can cut your vacation food bill by more than half.

15. Shop for meals at supermarkets. For breakfast, you can carry out yogurts, fruit, bagels, and donuts. Full-service supermarkets have great delis for lunch, and their fried chicken dinners are considerably less than KFC.

16. If you do have to book with a hotel, call the hotel directly and ask, "Can you quote me your best price?" or "Do you have any promotional rates during my stay?" Hotels are notorious for not quoting you the best price unless you ask for it.

LESSON OF THE DAY

Remember this as you sit with the peanuts-and-Coke crowd back in coach: the first-class passengers arrive only a split-second sooner than you.

Reach Out and Touch Someone—for Less

You can be dialing for dollars in no time

I have to admit it: AT&T, MCI, and Sprint have buffaloed me for years with a byzantine rate structure that has been so confusing, so full of smoke and mirrors, that I never knew if I was getting a good deal or not.

So I stuck with MCI for years, figuring at least I was receiving five frequent flier miles with American Airlines for every dollar I spent with MCI's "Friends and Family" pricing plan.

Then I saw a small newspaper ad for Telegroup, advertising cheap international rates. Since we frequently call Nicole's parents in Switzerland, we are price-sensitive on international rates. Telegroup was not only 40 percent cheaper (from 53-cents to 32 cents a minute), but we could call any time of day or night. MCI restricted the 53 cent rate to only weekends or before 8:00 A.M. weekdays. Otherwise, Swiss phone calls cost more than a buck a minute (ouch!). It wasn't hard saying *auf Weidersehn* to MCI.

Telegroup also has a great domestic rate plan. As long as I spend $50 a month (otherwise a $5 service charge kicks in), I can call anywhere in the U.S. at any time of day or night for *10.8¢ a minute.* Believe me, phoning my folks in California in the middle of the day has been a revelation, since it's been ingrained in my brain since I was a young boy to wait until 5:01 P.M. to dial long distance.

Now that I have Telegroup's 10.8 cent per minute rate in my pocket, I can see the telephone forest for the trees. AT&T, which owns 60 percent of the long-distance market, gets down to 12 cents a minute on weekends and late night on weekdays, but regular business hours cost a mint—around 25 cents a minute. Ditto for MCI and Sprint. It's tough to comparison shop, since all three companies offer various pricing plans that only a tax lawyer could decipher.

That's why I recommend going with a long-distance "reseller" such as Telegroup. These companies purchase network time from AT&T at a wholesale rate and resell it to customers. Lower overhead means lower rates. When AT&T began selling excess long distance capacity in 1989 they told Telegroup, "Since we're set up to do the billing, we'll handle it for you."

A funny thing happened: AT&T never billed customers for their long-distance charges with Telegroup. Their thinking was, *Without cash flow, these companies will go under.*

Telegroup managed to develop its own billing system before AT&T's wish became reality. But that's the way the long-distance game is played. This is a cutthroat business that rakes in $1 billion a year.

Advertisements are designed to mislead you. Perhaps you've seen those MCI ads offering "10 cents a minute." Well, you can get 10 cents a minute for only *one* phone number—for example, your parents'. Meanwhile, you'll pay 18 cents a minute for all your other calls. Another ad for Telecom, an MCI division, failed to mention that you receive their low, low rate only if your call lasts 20 minutes or more.

When I asked my phone rep, Bob Iverson of Telegroup, about all the shenanigans, all he could do was shake his head. "It's whoever can come up with the trickiest gimmick," said Bob. "It's like the gas wars in the 1960s."

I know what he means. I recently received a red, white, and blue "Xpress Delivery" packet in the mail, and inside was a $100 check made out to me from AT&T. When I cashed it, I would be automatically switched to AT&T's One Rate—15 cents a minute, 24 hours a day.

These days, you shouldn't have much difficulty finding something closer to 10 cents a minute, but you'll have to choose your poison. For me, it's the $5-a-month access charge with Telegroup if I fail to spend $50 a month. With our Swiss phone calls, we're covering that nut.

Perhaps your mailbox has been flooded with junk mail from some of the "dial-around" companies—where you dial an access code starting with 10 and 3 numbers, 1, and then the area code. VarTec Telecom pitches its "10811 DimeLine" rate, but there's a $5 a month access fee *and* a 3-minute minimum per call. In other words, your cheapest call will be 30 cents, and there is no incremental billing (more on that later).

To illustrate what a $5 access fee could mean to your total bill, let's say you make 60 minutes of long-distance calls in 1 month. At 10 cents a minute, you pay $6. Add the $5 access fee, and you're paying $11 for sixty minutes, or 18 cents a minute. Not the greatest deal.

Gabbing for hours brings the rate down considerably. If you make 4 hours of long distance calls in a month with DimeLine, that will cost you $24 plus $5, or a per minute rate of 12 cents—not bad. But don't forget that 3-minute minimum charge!

Other dial-around companies, such as VarTec, Telco, Matrix, and Telecom USA, advertise such blaring claims as "dial 10799 and save 68 percent" or "touch-tone 10457 and save 25 percent off AT&T basic rates."

Take a closer look. The 10457 Dial and Save company says a call from Denver to Dallas costs 30 cents per minute with AT&T during business hours, but only 22.5 cents with their company. Yes, that's cheaper than AT&T, but I'm paying 10.8 cents with Telegroup, so why should I switch? Even 10457's night-and-weekend rate of 12 cent per minute is 10 percent more than Telegroup.

Confused with all the numbers? Welcome to the club. As you sort out the phone company come-ons, keep these thoughts in mind:

- **Don't be afraid to switch.** Did you know that long-distance phone rates have fallen 40–47 percent in the last ten years? I didn't. There are a lot of people loyal to AT&T who are still paying 24 cents a minute because they've never shopped long distance. Become that shopper. Get in the game. I'm afraid I stayed with MCI too long.

- **Use Telegroup as a benchmark.** These days, I am paying 10.8 cents per minute, 24 hours a day. If your phone company can't beat that, then call Bob Iverson at (800) 338–0225, ext. 2547. "If you go with Telegroup and then find a company that offers you better rates than ours with better service, then we'll help you make the move," said Bob.

- **Check other long-distance resellers.** Let your fingers do the walking. Call Unidial (800–895–7474), LCI (800–524–4685), American Travel Net (800–477–9692), or Trans National (800–653–2669). Be sure to ask about monthly minimums. Of the "dial-around" companies, 10502 Talk Cents (800–569–8700) appears to be the best, with a rate of 9 cents a minute and a $4.95 monthly access fee.

- **Look for "incremental" billing.** Nearly all phone companies bill on a "per-minute" rate. Thus, if you call an old college friend in Miami, get her answering machine, and hang up immediately, you're still charged for a full minute.

  Telegroup, on the other hand, charges for every 6 seconds, which means I'm billed 1 cent for every 6 seconds. If my phone call is 10 minutes and 8 seconds, I'm charged for 10 minutes and 12 seconds, not 11 minutes. I didn't think incremental billing would make a difference, but it's saving me 5 to 10 bucks a month. Those little increments add up.

- **Know that calling in-state could be higher than calling out-of-state.** Low-population states, like my Colorado and New Mexico, have very high in-state rates. Why does it cost more to call from Colorado Springs to Denver than it does to call New York City? The answer has something to do with politics. (Are you surprised?) High-population states such as California and Ohio have lower rates.

- **Don't fall for the cell-phone bait.** A local supermarket was offering *free* digital cellular phones, but that's like getting free initiation dues at a health club: The idea is to get you inside the door and start collecting a monthly fee from you. Cell phones are getting cheaper by the year, but they still cost more than $50 a month for minimal use. Is it really worth $600 a year to have a cell phone in the car?

- **Finally, watch the rates on those prepaid phone cards.** I think prepaid cards are great for travelers. I've seen 100 minutes for $16.99 at Sam's Club, which is 17 cents a minute—very good.

  But don't fall for the come-on deals as I did. I purchased an MCI prepaid card. Wrong! When I read the fine print, I was paying nearly 30 cents a minute. While I expect prices to come down on prepaid phone cards, the rates vary widely. But why should I be surprised?

There's a lot of static when it comes to shopping long-distance, but let your fingers do the walking—to one of the phone resellers or dial-around companies!

DAY 18

Giving It the Old College Try

College is expensive, but if there's a will there could be a way

When *Pastor's Family* magazine published "College or Bust" not long ago, a pastor's wife, Yvonne Jones, told me that she "devoured" the article.

I know what Yvonne means. Ask any parent of a high school student about college, and you'll receive a blank look of desperation on his or her face. With a ninth-grader and an eighth-grader in my household, I'm already losing sleep. *How are we going to pay for our children's college educations?*

I'm sure my parents tossed and turned as well, but back in the 1970s, colleges weren't asking for the fatted calf—and the rest of the herd—for Junior to attend their institution of higher learning. Although my out-of-state tuition costs at the University of Oregon stretched my parents, I graduated without owing anyone a nickel. That means that during my first few post-college years I was able to do some fun things (like live and work at a California ski resort) before "settling down."

There are no ski-bum days ahead for Andrea and Patrick: the stakes are too high. Fifteen years ago the typical college-educated worker made 38 percent more than a worker with a high school diploma. Today, the typical college-educated worker makes 73 percent more.

There's another issue at work. I want Andrea to marry a college-educated young man who can earn enough to allow her to be a stay-at-home mom when the kids arrive. I want Patrick to be able to adequately provide for his family as well. A college education greatly increases the chances of that happening.

THE STEEP RISE IN TUITION

It doesn't do any good to bellyache about it, but college tuition has risen at more than *double* the increases in the general cost of living. In the past 15 years tuition has almost tripled. If you have your heart set on sending Joshua to Harvard next year, the 4-year cost will be $120,000. If he stays close to home, a 4-year education at a state school averages $37,140.

Why so much? Because many parents have decided that the more expensive the tuition, the better the degree. And educators have caught on to this phenomenon: *Hey, parents are willing to shell out for prestige. They'll pay just about anything.*

I'm sorry, but it's not my goal in life to witness Andrea and Patrick's graduation from an Ivy League school. In fact, I strongly believe that sending children to a Christian college may be the most important decision parents have to make as their children enter young adulthood.

But a good Christian university—like Wheaton College, for example—is closing in on the $20,000-a-year mark. What if Andrea's heart's desire is to attend Wheaton or Samford University or Biola University?

I'll have to think about that one. But I know one thing: as much as I've saved by being a good shopper, I still don't have an extra $1,500 lying around *each month* to invest in a college fund, which is what money managers say I should be doing for a 13-year-old child. Instead, I'm going to be looking for deals. Grove University in Pennsylvania, for instance, is a small Christian liberal arts school that charges around $8,500 a year for everything—tuition, room, and board, and they even throw in a laptop computer. Sterling College, a Christian college in Sterling, Kansas, charges $9,500 for tuition, room, and board.

Inexpensive colleges—we're talking "relative" here—can be found. You need to hunt them down, as well as hunt down financial scholarships—not financial aid—since scholarships, grants, and fellowships do not have to be repaid. In our case, we'll play up our children's talents (tennis and languages) and look for every obscure grant we can find ("the Swiss-American Good Citizen Award"). We'll surf the Internet looking for scholarships as well (*web.studentservices.com/fastweb* searches more than 200,000 scholarships, grants, and loans).

We'll also be negotiating a good deal. Often, the quoted price of tuition—say, $13,000 a year—is no more believable than a sticker price on a shiny new Lexus. Many schools are willing to drop several thousand dollars off the base price to get Johnny into their school. A good friend of mine was able to send his oldest child to a college in the Pacific Northwest after the school cut a deal to slash tuition from $20,000 to $9,000 a year. The parents prevailed because they were persistent with the financial aid office.

Remember, the number of college freshmen is down 14 percent from a decade ago, so the laws of supply and demand should be working in our favor—except for Stanford and the elite schools. There are still too many parents willing to pay any price, bear any burden, to have their child graduate from a prestigious college.

Here are some other college-bound strategies to remember:

- **Shy away from prepaid tuition programs**. While plans vary in details, the family pays into a state program a set amount of money each month based on the age of the child. The state then invests the money and guarantees that the child's 4-year tuition costs will be paid at any state public institution, regardless of how much tuition rates may rise.

   I don't like prepaid plans for several reasons, the biggest being that it takes the option of Christian higher education right out of our hands. Family situations change; do you know for sure where you will be living in a decade? The Institute of Certified Financial Planners, which studied various state programs, said that disciplined investors can do better investing that monthly amount on their own.

- **Talk to your son or daughter about your expectations**. Growing up, I always heard that college life was 50 percent study and 50 percent social. I doubt we'll be sending Andrea and Patrick to any "party schools." No, they will have to buckle down.

   The days of taking a year off and traipsing through Europe with a Eurail Pass and a backpack went out with Woodstock. The goal is to *get in and get out*. This is not a harsh policy but rather a recognition that a vast majority of college students do *not* return once they quit school.

- **Ask them to take advanced placement tests.** This was the *best* thing I did in high school, and it saved my parents and me one year of college. I took AP tests in several subjects, which helped me enter college with thirty credits, or two-thirds of a school year. Even though I had to work hard my last year, averaging eighteen units per semester, I graduated from the University of Oregon in three years and saved my parents a bundle.

Several schools are offering three-year degree programs even if they don't take advanced placement. Check out *College Board Index of Majors and Graduate Degrees* at your library or local bookstore. Drury University in Springfield, Missouri, and Albertus Magnus University in New Haven, Connecticut, offer three-year degrees.

Your children can also earn college credit through the International Baccalaureate program offered at some high schools, and through College Level Examination Placement (CLEP) tests, a national program that tests for proficiency in several subject areas.

- **Take a "video" tour of the college.** Sure, you'll want to personally visit your child's top choice or two, but you can whittle down your options by contacting Collegiate Choice (201–871–0098). Their video tours are fifty minutes long and cost $15.
- **Don't seek early admission.** If your child decides early, you can't play off one college's financial aid or scholarship program against another.
- **Ask the kids to attend a community college for a year or two.** Tuition fees are not only lower, but you can save money by having your college student live at home. Use that savings to fund the final two years at an out-of-town school.
- **Ask the kids to work.** If earning several thousand dollars a year is the difference between taking on college loans or graduating from college debt-free, send them to work. They will also appreciate their education more and learn the value of gainful employment.
- **Somehow, by hook or by crook, get them through without incurring debt.** Whether the kids have to commute from home, Nicole has to take on a full-time job, I work overtime, or the kids participate in a work-study program, that's the way it will be.

- **If you have to get a loan, do everything you can to pay it off before graduation.** The worst-case scenario is taking out a home-equity loan or refinancing your mortgage, since that will be a financial setback. Borrowing against your retirement plan is another option, although there could be a major tax penalty. Some retirement plans allow you to borrow your pretax dollars as long as you repay in a certain time period—usually five years.
- **Encourage summer school.** If tuition is cheaper during the summer, why not go? And what about taking summer classes at your community college? Just make sure that credits are transferable.
- **Encourage summer internships.** Interns may work for peanuts, but it's a great way to make contacts for that first post-college job.

LESSON OF THE DAY

Paying for college is a daunting prospect, but it has been done. Just remember to give it the "old college try."

DAY 19

Losing Money Any Way You Can

Gambling, get-rich-quick schemes, and risky investments will separate you from your cash faster than you can say "Lotto"

When I fill my gas tank on Wednesday night at my corner Quik Mart, there's always a line waiting for me at the checkout stand.

Oh, yeah. It's Lotto night.

Colorado, like 41 other states and the District of Columbia, has a lottery, and state-sponsored gambling has become as American as apple pie. Our governments pitch Lotto and Powerball as though it's our civic duty to pull out our wallets and play their games of chance. But that's not all: casino gambling is expanding, floating gaming parlors are back on the Mississippi River, and sports betting is commonplace.

I can offer two compelling reasons why gambling is a bad bet. One, it's not biblical. While there are not any "Thou shalt nots" in the Bible regarding roulette or scratch-off games, gambling does violate several major themes in Scripture:

- Gambling encourages greed (Luke 12:15; Heb. 13:5; 1 Tim. 6:10).
- Gambling encourages materialism and discontent (1 Tim. 6:9; Ps. 62:10).
- Gambling discourages honest labor (Prov. 28:19; 13:11).
- Gambling encourages "get rich quick" thinking (Prov. 28:20).
- Gambling encourages reckless investment of God-given resources (Matt. 25:14–30).

Second, you're practically guaranteed that you will lose your money. The sorry truth is that the odds of winning a million-dollar jackpot from the state are astronomical—around 14 million to 1. That's the same odds as for my golfing a hole-in-one.

Don't think you can improve your odds by playing slots, roulette, craps, or blackjack. Sooner or later, the "house" will take your hard-earned money—sometimes with a smile and sometimes without.

So please, do yourself a favor and stay away from gambling. God will honor your obedience, and you can spend your money on things with a more worthwhile return—such as Christian education for your children.

Another thing to flee is Internet porn. My research tells me that virtual sex is one of the few industries actually making money on the Internet.

Pornography is addictive, but even an innocent word search can take you down paths you never thought possible. Let's say you wanted to find the book *Little Women*. A word search could direct you to a porn site with pictures of short, naked women, all for $19.95 per peep session.

If porn is part of your life, will you talk to your pastor or a trusted friend? Not only can you clean up your thought life, but you won't be spending money where you shouldn't.

MULTILEVEL MARKETING

In the last year, Nicole and I were invited to an Amway presentation. I think we had been roped into one the first year of our marriage, but this time we were a bit curious since some good friends asked us to come.

I have nothing against Amway; its products are top-notch. The founder and president, Richard DeVos, is a wonderful Christian man and a philanthropist. Even if you never get into the multilevel marketing aspect of Amway, you could save some nice change by buying everything from corn flakes to chain saws from their beautiful catalogs.

What I would like to address is the general concept of multilevel marketing found in Amway, Excel long distance, NSA JuicePlus, Shaklee vitamins, among others. After our evening of hearing the Amway pitch, I went home and typed out this list for Nicole:

PROS AND CONS REGARDING MULTILEVEL MARKETING

Pros

1. Make money (maybe).

Cons

1. You have to look at every person you know or every person you become friends with as a potential customer. It's always in the back of your mind: "Is this someone I can tell about my business?" It never leaves your brain.
2. You never really ever "do" anything. You are just trying to get someone to sign up so that he can get someone to sign up so that he can get someone to sign up.
3. You have to put in many hours with no guarantee you'll make anything.

4. I feel called to a writing ministry with magazines and books. Why do I want to go in this direction with my limited amount of off-hours? Is this what God would have me do?

5. In the Christian community, how does talking up this particular business reflect on me?

6. The goal is to build my own pyramid. I get six or seven people, who in turn get six or seven people, and so forth. Is this what I want to do with my life?

7. I really *enjoy* the life God has given me. I really *enjoy* my work. I can't wait to go to work many mornings. I don't enjoy selling or trying to talk someone into something they don't necessarily need. Why do I want to do this?

8. I like the two of us being known as "Mike and Nicole Yorkey." Do I want to be known as "Mike and Nicole Yorkey, those Amway (or Shaklee or Excel or whatever) people"?

9. Working a multilevel business would involve many evenings away from home. It would take me away from my family, whom I don't see enough anyway.

10. Why would Nicole want to do this? Is she suited to sales? (I don't think so.)

11. Looking back, we can say that the Lord has always provided us enough money to live on. In fact, we can say that the Lord has blessed us financially in tremendous ways. It's always been enough. If God wants us to have more money, shouldn't we rely on him? After all, he's been there every step of the way for us.

ABOUT PONZI SCHEMES

Investment frauds—also know as pyramid or Ponzi schemes— have been around since Ramses II sat on his Egyptian throne. The principle is that hundreds of Peters pay a few Pauls, and those on top of the pyramid walk away rich.

I unsuspectingly walked into one very recently after reading a two-column newspaper ad that said, "How to Pay for College Without Going Broke!" A free seminar promised that I would learn how to "avoid using up savings for college costs" and "build a five-figure college fund without investing."

I know that when something sounds too good to be true, then it is too good to be true. But I had to see for myself.

I strode into the darkened high-school auditorium where I saw another fifty parents. On stage, a slick, computerized slide show began, with the narrator describing the dire straits families find themselves in when it comes to paying for a college education.

The narrator had a solution: the Kids in College Educational Network, a company he founded. In a nutshell, parents who join Kids in College (by paying an annual $95 "administration" fee) receive credit in a trust account when they—or anyone they "sponsor"—spend money at an associated business. Forty percent of each contribution to the trust fund goes directly to the family's college account. The other 60 percent is divided among the college accounts of five other families in the program. Miss an annual fee, and you lose all your credit.

This smelled like a classic pyramid scheme, which the speaker didn't try to hide. In fact, he said there were "good pyramids" and "bad pyramids"; good pyramids represented by a family tree or a corporate ladder, and bad pyramids in which unsuspecting investors are fleeced.

If I signed up tonight, he intoned, I would be Number 315 in the pyramid, and all those "below" me would be helping pay for my children's college education, *so if you act now* . . . .

I credit the speaker for admitting that he was *numero uno* in the pyramid, but an hour was all I could take. When I left the auditorium, I was "intercepted" by another KIC salesman. He asked me why I didn't want to sign up. I hate being asked questions like that.

I drove home thinking, *Lord, I don't know how we're going to pay for college, but I'd rather rely on you and not that guy on stage.* And that's the bottom line to this book: we have no idea what our financial futures hold. Our economy could collapse, the stock market could become worthless in a week, our retirement accounts could vanish, and our dollars could be devalued. If any of those scenarios were to happen, widespread panic would rule the streets.

Those of us who have our financial houses in order, who are used to living within our means and know how to stretch a buck, will be in a better position to provide for our families. It's when we get off track, and chase investment scams, that we can start losing money any way we can.

Put another way, we are "salary men," and we know nothing about shaky investment "opportunities" such as penny stocks, precious metals, highly leveraged real estate, and oil and gas ventures.

How do you avoid these and many other investment schemes? The Institute for Certified Financial Planners says to never invest over the telephone. Avoid "buy-now" sales pitches. Be wary of outrageous promises, such as excessively high interest rates, 50-to-1 returns on real estate, or a 500 percent profit on oil and gas investments.

Instead, stick with more traditional means of investing, such as stocks, bonds, and mutual funds.

LESSON OF THE DAY

If someone promises to double your money, it probably means that he or she is promising to double their *money.*

I'll Take Odds and Ends for $50, Alex

Quick-hitting tips that don't fit elsewhere

Today I'm going to cover some brief money-saving ideas that I couldn't include elsewhere in the book.

TIP

Your local cineplex is showing the latest, everyone's-talking-about-it blockbuster, but it's rated PG-13. Is it suitable viewing for your two teenagers and one middle-school child? You're not sure, but with their pleas ringing in your ears, off you go. The cost for the entire family is $32.50, which doesn't include a stop at the snack bar.

A half-hour into the film, it's apparent that this was one blockbuster everyone could have done without. Double-entendre jokes abound, and the "love interests" hop in bed because they just met each other ten minutes ago. The violence is memorable and graphic. If only you had known.

Well, you can know. *Preview*, which reviews the latest Hollywood releases from a Christian perspective, is published twice monthly. I've been reading this newsletter for seven years, and it's helped us avoid some real stinkers. Cost is $33 a year. Write Preview, 1309 Seminole Dr., Richardson, TX 75080, or phone 214–231–9910.

Last movie tip: Even the best films end up at the $1.75 houses before too long, so be patient.

TIP

Don't clip coupons just for grocery shopping. I never make an oil change at one of those 10-minute places without a coupon, and I love miniature-golf coupons found in newspapers and junk mail.

TIP

You've got to get a bread machine. With prices for good machines now under $150, there isn't any reason not to. All it takes is setting a timer, pouring in two cups of flour, adding a little yeast and a few other ingredients, and fresh, hot bread is in your mouth less than three hours later.

TIP

What's the best consumer magazine? It's still *Consumer Reports* ($24 a year for 12 issues; write P.O. Box 51166, Boulder, CO 80323–1166). The magazine, founded in 1936, has changed with the times, which means you'll catch a whiff of political correctness on the pages. But what's uncanny is how often *CR* has the right story on the right product, from tires to computers to vacuum cleaners.

What's the best "frugal living" newsletter? I vote for Mary Hunt's *Cheapskate Monthly* (562–630–8845). Crammed with advice and a "Tiptionary" column of reader tips, this 12-page monthly resource is $18 a year.

══════════════════════════════════════ TIP

Buy your jewelry and kid's musical instruments at pawn shops. Don't laugh, but pawn shops (at least in my neck of the woods) have gone upscale. Shirts and ties have replaced biker's leather, and dank stores have given way to brightly lit displays. Jewelry and musical instruments are half off and sometimes more—a lot more.

We purchased Patrick's alto saxophone for $385 when music stores were asking $1,200 new or $45 a month for a rental.

Most pawn shops have jewelers appraise the more expensive diamonds (since they don't want to get ripped off, either), and they have sophisticated machines in-house to grade gold content. As a fifteenth-anniversary wedding present, Nicole picked out a beautiful 18K gold necklace for $300 when similar necklaces were going for $1,000 in mall jewelry stores. And I can't tell you about the gold jewelry my mother-in-law purchased at a pawn store. She'd kill me!

(Psst! Here's what happened. My mother-in-law, Thea Schmied, saw a beautiful gold bracelet in Vail for $3,600, which was hopelessly overpriced. Two days later at a Colorado Springs pawn shop she bought a nearly identical 18K gold bracelet for $300. I don't think anyone in her native Switzerland will be the wiser!)

══════════════════════════════════════ TIP

Use your camcorder (or a friend's) to film your valuables. This filmed record will come in handy in case your house is lost in a catastrophic event. After years of procrastinating, we finally videoed our house and valuables a couple of years ago and sent a copy of the tape to my parents for safekeeping.

TIP

Personal computers have fallen under the $1,000 ceiling, and if all you're using your home computer for is e-mail, the kid's homework, and Internet access, you don't need a $3,000 state-of-the-art model.

Used computers can be found on the Internet, but that would be too risky for me. My final advice: buy a Mac. I know Apple has been in financial trouble, but after working with both platforms, the Apple Macintosh is easier to use.

TIP

Is there a moving day in your future? Some companies, like North American Van Lines (800–348–2111), have a "You Load, We Drive" program in which the big rig rolls into your street, and it's your responsibility to get your boxes and furniture to the truck, where the driver loads it.

I've hired husky high school kids to do the heavy lifting, and they were very conscientious, not like some of the "professional" movers I've seen. In a *Consumer Reports* survey, 55 percent reported that paid movers damaged their goods, compared to 32 percent who moved on their own.

You can save up to *half* on an interstate move by loading yourself but leaving the driving to someone else.

TIP

If you are pregnant, make every friend aware that you're in the "family way." Many moms are looking for a good opportunity to give away their maternity and infants' clothes to a good home.

TIP

Do-it-yourself. Granted, there is a trade-off between time versus money, but there are some things you and the family could do around the house that could pay for a nice vacation.

- New lawn mowers—self-propelled models that "mulch" the grass so you don't have to bag it—are worth the investment. I can mow our rather large lawn in 40 minutes, saving me a $20 bill over some lawn service.
- Don't do windows? That'll cost you another $50 to $100. Our house has more than 50 windows, and it's Nicole who often draws window duty, but on those occasions I say, "Thanks, sweetie. You saved us $100 today."
- Are you a messie? About 10 percent of all U.S. households use a maid or housecleaning service. These maids must use a golden dust mop, because they charge anywhere from $75 to $250 per day. On the other hand, if I were cleaning someone else's dirt and grime, I'd charge double that amount.

  If you *have* to have housecleaning because you're a two-income household or physically not up to it, call a local high school and ask if a teen would be interested in doing some housework. Paying a 16-year-old $6 or $7 an hour to run a vacuum, scrub toilets, and polish furniture is more than she could earn at McDonald's and cheaper than those Merry Maid services.

- Next, wash your own clothes. You may laugh, but Laundromats are moving into the suburbs and finding a lot of customers. "One of the fastest-growing segments in our industry is the wash/dry/fold service," says Brian Wallace, director of communications for the Coin Laundry Association. "People can bring in their dirty laundry and pick it up later, all clean and folded."

You're paying a clean penny to have someone else do your laundry. Nicole and I have folded our share of laundry after 10:00 P.M., bleary-eyed and ready for bed, but we're willing to do it ourselves.

TIP

If your package has to absolutely, positively, be there tomorrow, always check Fed Ex's P.M. box for afternoon delivery. The "overnight morning" service usually delivers packages to businesses by 9:00 A.M., and the "afternoon" delivery arrives by 11:00 A.M. Can your package wait two hours?

TIP

Never dial a number that begins with the 900 prefix. Not only will this call be your nickel, it will also be your dollar—lots of them. Especially watch out for junk-mail solicitations that urge you to call a certain 900 number to win your prize vacation. That scam could cost you a $29.95 phone call!

TIP

Have you ever heard of Coolhunt? It's an esoteric marketing science of tracking what "cool kids in major American cities are thinking and doing and buying," said an article in *The New Yorker*.

The upshot is, street chic "trickles up" to become the fashion fad of the moment, which is why Nike and Reebok are coming out with new sneakers every season—not once a year as in the past.

Carry an attitude that your family doesn't have to have the latest fashion. In fact, laugh at the absurdity!

=== TIP

Make your second car a beater. Better yet, make your second car a beater truck. I drive a 15-year-old GMC S-15 pickup with 130,000 miles, and I couldn't be happier. If it gets a dent, I don't care. I've saved delivery charges by hauling my own topsoil, sod, and flowers, and my truck has sure come in handy when I've had to take my lawn mower to the repair shop.

=== TIP

We've seen fads come and go through the years: pet rocks, mood rings, disco dancing, but every Christmas some toy becomes the gotta-have-it sensation. I remember being in San Diego a couple of Christmases ago when Tickle-Me-Elmos were *the* thing. Two days before Christmas I counted 123 classified ads selling Tickle-Me-Elmos for inflated prices in the *San Diego Union Tribune*. Ridiculous!

=== TIP

And finally, you can save money after you're in heaven. The average funeral costs $4,000, and much of that comes from the casket or coffin, which has an average retail price of $3,000. Your dead body doesn't need to be entombed in a silk-lined casket.

I admit that it would be pretty creepy to call Direct Casket (800–772–2753) or The Down to Earth Coffin Company (603–444–5874) and "shop" for my own casket, but it might make sense. In addition, let your loved ones know that they don't have to spend an arm and a leg on your funeral (sorry, bad joke).

There are zillions of money-saving tips,
so if one of these ideas looks good,
photocopy it and file for later use.

The Checkout Lane

Making saving money a lifestyle

It's our final day, the time to wrap things up. Remember Mahlon Hetrick, the Christian financial counselor who opened this book with his observations about budgeting?

I'd like to finish with a short question-and-answer time with Mahlon. Here goes:

> Q: **How do you feel about debt consolidation? If you're a family drowning in debt, this seems like a chance to roll all your debts into one loan. The interest is tax deductible since you're borrowing against the equity in your home. For many, it's the only way to get back on their financial feet again.**
>
> Mahlon: I was in the banking business for thirty years, and I saw hundreds of people come back asking for a consolidation loan after we had given them one only two years earlier! Loan consolidations, home-equity loans, lines of credit—whatever you call them— didn't solve the problem.

If they were mismanaging their money in the first place, then all a consolidation loan did was give them more money to mismanage. Whenever I asked people to define their problem, they never defined their real problem, which was ignorance about managing their money and wrong attitudes about spending and use of credit. More money did not solve their problems.

Q: **What were some of those wrong attitudes?**

Mahlon: Pride and greed are the two greatest problems that lead to money difficulties. The world's attitude is, *Whoever ends up with the most toys wins.* Couples want to win that race, so they start gathering their toys whether they can afford them or not. And that's how they end up with a money problem.

People have a hard time admitting they're greedy or proud, but most are willing to confess they lack discipline. If people can look deep in their hearts and admit their shortcomings, they will end up with a greater joy, peace, and understanding about their finances. They will discover God's ways when they are obedient to him.

Q: **What are God's ways?**

Mahlon: Proverbs 3:9 says we should honor the Lord by giving him the first part of all of our income. Proverbs 21:2 says we can justify our every deed, but God looks at our motives. For instance, is our motive for tithing to honor the Lord? If so, then our motives are pure.

Dr. Harold Fickett, onetime pastor of First Baptist Church in Van Nuys, California, once said that if his entire congregation went on welfare and immediately commenced tithing 10 percent, the income of the church would triple. What a chastisement! We want God's blessings and the joy of the Lord, but we don't want to do what he says.

In addition to honoring the Lord, God wants us to give to the needy. Look at 2 Corinthians 9:7–9: "Don't force anyone to give more than he really wants to, for cheerful givers are the ones God prizes. God is able to make it up to you by giving you everything you need and more, so that there will not only be enough for your own needs, but plenty left over to give joyfully to others. It is as the Scriptures say: 'The godly man gives generously to the poor. His good deeds will be an honor to him forever'" (TLB).

After fifteen years of being a Christian financial counselor, I have heard testimony after testimony of people who chose to honor the Lord in their giving, and when they did, the blessings started coming.

Q: But if I give my money away, how will I get ahead?

Mahlon: God says, with the same measure you give, it will be returned to you, shaken down and overflowing. I've talked to many pastors, and none of them ever had a course in seminary on the theology of stewardship or money matters. Few people realize that God's Word has more to say about finances than anything else except love, and I know that surprises some people. When we put God first in our budgets, God blesses our obedience. We are in the obedience department; he is in the blessing department.

Q: Would you say that couples who are tens of thousands of dollars in debt, with collection agencies hounding them day and night, shouldn't get a loan consolidation?

Mahlon: No, I'm not saying that at all. I've seen consolidation loans work when the couples have learned how to put together, analyze, organize, and control a budget. We need to overcome our ignorance with wisdom, and wisdom comes from God. Proverbs 2:6 says, "For the Lord grants wisdom."

If you choose to be a good manager, God has good news for you: He will return a blessing far greater than expected. God wants us to enjoy what he entrusts to us.

Well, we've spent 21 days looking at hundreds of ways to save money on just about anything. As we come to a finish, let me sum up the "take away" value of this book:

1. Give to the Lord. Let's go back to 2 Corinthians 9 (TLB). The first part of verse 7 says, "Everyone must make up his own mind as to how much he should give" (TLB). It's been said before, but it bears repeating: It's impossible to outgive God. That lesson was driven home to me recently when my old truck began knocking like crazy. One shop told me that the engine was shot and that I should think about buying a new car.

Something told me I should get a second opinion. I asked around work, and a colleague suggested trying a Christian car repair shop she had used. I took the truck in, and they confirmed that it had a bad bearing and the engine needed to be replaced. The repair estimate came to $2,400.

This was early December, not a great time for a sizable repair bill. It was also a time when we were doing our year-end giving to our church and missionaries we support. I gulped and authorized the repair work.

The next day I received a phone call.

"Are you ready for some good news?" asked the mechanic.

"This time of year, yes," I replied.

"You know, I never did feel right about our diagnosis, so I asked another mechanic from our downtown shop to drop by and look at your truck. We discovered that your knocking sound was coming from the transmission. You don't need a new engine, just a new transmission. We can fix your car for $1,400."

Hallelujah! I felt like the Lord had reached down and put $1,000 into my pocket.

2. Know where your money is going. Even if you have no intention of *following* a budget, at least create one so you know whether you're breaking even, falling deeper into debt, or putting aside a little each month. Too many families have *no idea* that they are overspending each month. Do you?

3. Tuck something away for retirement, especially if you're past 40 years of age. Financial counselors will tell you that you should have opened a retirement account back in your twenties, but the kids started arriving and you were trying to buy that first home. Fine, you did what you had to do. Now you have to start saving before it's too late. Too many economists are predicting that Social Security will not be there by the time we reach retirement age, and even if it is, Social Security will not replace your income or provide for all your retirement needs.

4. Pay your credit card balance in full each month. Please heed this advice. You can't save for retirement and invest any of your hard-earned money until your Visa slate is clean.

5. If you have a few dollars left over each month, invest it in your house. I don't have any money lying around to play the stock market or gold futures, for which I'm grateful, since the financial markets are best left to the pros. (I've seen stories about monkeys throwing darts at a Standard & Poor's 500 board and outperforming the Wall Street experts.)

I'm a big believer in throwing a few extra dollars each month against my mortgage, thus saving tons of money in interest and paying off my loan much sooner than 30 years. Marc Eisenson, author of *The Banker's Secret* (914–758–1400), is the expert on prepaying loans.

6. Having your financial house in order means you're in a better position to respond to needs. If you've sponsored a Compassion Child or dug down deep to help your church send a missionary team to Russia, you know what a great feeling it is to participate in God's work.

7. Finally, make this saving-money thing a lifestyle. Believe me, it's better to go through life experiencing peace and contentment about your finances than to struggle with worry, frustration, or fear. Having a peace about your finances is worth more than any Powerball jackpot.

LESSON OF THE DAY

Now that you're ready to save money right and left, you should pick up another book in this series called 21 Days to Financial Freedom *(available 4/98) by my colleague Dan Benson. This excellent resource is bursting with ideas on how to get out and stay out of debt and how to invest more successfully. Give it a read!*